CHRIST
The Fullness of God

Devotional Thoughts on Colossians & Philemon

Christ
The Fullness of God

Cornerstone Christian Church
608 N Bartlett
Medford OR 97501
USA

Published in the United States as A Cornerstone Publication
ISBN-9798870399492

Table of Contents

About the Author

Stan Way (B.S., Pastoral Theology, Bethany University) has been in Christian ministry for over fifty five years and is currently serving as Pastor Emeritus of Cornerstone Christian Church in Medford, Oregon. He is also an ordained Minister of the Word in the federation of United Reformed Churches in North America.

Preface

It amazes me how contemporary ancient writings can be. Paul's letter to the Colossians was written while he was in prison in Rome (c. A.D. 60). Even though he had never visited Colossae, he was very concerned about the Gnostic ideas that false teachers were trying to mix with true Apostolic teaching and pervert the gospel message. The church today faces the same challenges. We have to push back against teachings that distort the pure gospel. This is the obligation of every generation of Christian believers. The Gnostic ideas that deny the deity of Christ and call into question his redemptive work are still present with us. What we find in the book of Colossians will help us stand against the pressures of false teaching and remain faithful followers of Christ.

Colossians is a public letter to be read to the Christians in Colossae and the believers in Laodicea, while Philemon is a private Apostolic note sent to Paul's personal friend. Thankfully both have been preserved because they give us instruction that is theologically sound and practically applicational.

This small book is based on a series of sermons I preached at Cornerstone Christian Church in 2010. I think you will sense the pastoral nature of the book as you read it. The book isn't an academic work, it's more devotional. My prayer is that it will enrich your biblical understanding and deepen your devotion to Christ.

Stan Way
2023

Introduction

We live in a cultural environment that is hostile to the gospel and resists any religious claims that are exclusive and considered intolerant of other religious understandings. This presents us with some particular challenges as Christians striving to remain faithful to the gospel in this cultural climate. We're often confronted with the mixing of religious ideas and a hesitancy to make exclusive claims. We're pressured to soften our understanding of Christ's uniqueness and look for shared themes and complimentary ideas found in various religious systems. It's also assumed that religious convictions are essentially subjective and pragmatic, and only apply to those who believe them and find them to work for them. So, all religious ideas have equal merit. In this environment no one religious system should be seen as universal and objectively true to the exclusion of all others...they're all true!

Apparently this same attitude threatened the church in Colossae. The crucial question is: how do we combat this attitude? Are we to argue against every point of belief of every religious system? No. We're to lift up Christ and enlarge our knowledge of who he is and what he did. We're to develop a more full-bodied understanding of the gospel. The book of Colossians will help us do this.

CONTEXT

The first task is to establish the context of the book's writing. It's important that we attempt to read the letter through the eyes of the original readers, understanding that we're reading only one side of a conversation. There are three questions we need to address: what do we know about Colossae and its people; what's the condition of the church in Colossae; and what's the nature of the Colossian error? Regarding the city of Colossae, we know that it was prominent and prosperous as late as the fifth century B.C., and was referred to as 'a great city of Phrygia' (modern day Turkey). However, in Paul's day it was a city in decline, overshadowed by its sister cities, Laodica and Hierapolis. And yet, it remained a cosmopolitan city with a mixed population, culturally and religiously diverse, composed of various Gentile people groups and a significant number of Jews. Like other cosmopolitan cities, Colossae was a center of philosophical and religious conversation. Ideas were readily discussed, embraced, and mixed. The church in Colossae was striving to remain faithful to Christ and the gospel in this very demanding intellectual climate. At this point, the church appears to be faithful but threatened by error. Epaphras, the founding pastor of the church, went to Paul who was in prison in Rome, to report on the progress of the churches in the Lycus Valley, and also to seek Paul's counsel regarding how he could best protect his people from the theological error that confronted them.

Made up predominantly of Gentile converts, the church in Colossae was a small house church. Bishop J.B. Lightfoot made this observation: "Without doubt Colossae was the least important church to which any epistle of St. Paul is addressed."[1] And yet, the book is thoughtful, theologically rich, and filled with real pastoral concern. Church size seems to be

1   Lightfoot, J. B., *The Colossian Heresy,* (Scholars Press, Missoula, Mont., 1973), p. 16.

of no concern to Paul. His focus was on Christian believers. He expressed this when he wrote to the Corinthians - "…. there is the daily pressure on me of my anxiety for all the churches (2 Cor.11:28)." Reflected in the rich content of this letter is the Apostle's concern for a small group of Christians he had never met living in an insignificant city.

COLOSSIAN ERROR

When it comes to identifying the 'Colossian error' there is no detailed description of it. The clearest description we have is found in chapter 2 in which the contours of the error can be established through inference - *"See to it that no one takes you captive by philosophy and empty deceit, according to human tradition, according to the elemental spirits of the world, and not according to Christ. For in him the whole fullness of deity dwells bodily, and you have been filled in him, who is the head of all rule and authority. In him also you were circumcised with a circumcision made without hands, by putting off the body of the flesh, by the circumcision of Christ, having been buried with him in baptism, in which you were also raised with him through faith in the powerful working of God, who raised him from the dead. And you, who were dead in your trespasses and the uncircumcision of your flesh, God made alive together with him, having forgiven us all our trespasses, by canceling the record of debt that stood against us with its legal demands. This he set aside, nailing it to the cross. He disarmed the rulers and authorities and put them to open shame, by triumphing over them in him. Therefore let no one pass judgment on you in questions of food and drink, or with regard to a festival or a new moon or a Sabbath. These are a shadow of the things to come, but the substance belongs to Christ. Let no one disqualify you, insisting on asceticism and worship of angels, going on in detail about visions, puffed* up without reason by his sensuous mind, and not holding fast to the Head, from whom the whole body, nourished and knit together through its joints and ligaments, grows with a growth that is from God. If with Christ you died to the elemental spirits of the world, why, as if you were still alive in the world, do you submit to regulations— "Do not handle, Do not taste, Do not touch" (referring to things that all perish as they are used)— according to human precepts and teachings? These have indeed an appearance of wisdom in promoting self-made religion and asceticism and severity to the body, but they are of no value in stopping the indulgence of the flesh (Col.2:8-23).

ERROR IDENTIFIERS

Here are some identifiers of the error that can be drawn out of the text. First, Paul places it in the category of 'deceptive philosophy' - "See to it that no one takes you captive by philosophy and empty deceit,...(v.2:8)." In verse 2:4 he refers to the teaching as 'plausible arguments.' This suggests that the teaching was a coherent system of beliefs that was intellectually appealing. Very often aberrant teaching is like this, it appeals to the intellectual and spiritual pride of people. Second, the source of the teaching was 'human imagination', not divine revelation. It was based on 'human tradition' (v.2:8), or the ideas of man that were ultimately demonic in nature - "according to the elemental spirits of the world,...(v.2:8)." The teaching denigrated Christ, it was - "not according to Christ" - it wasn't Christ centered as the pure gospel is. Instead, it promoted ascetic disciplines, dietary restrictions, and the celebration of certain holy days (vv.16 & 18). Also, the teaching involved the veneration and worship of spiritual beings - "Let no one disqualify you, insisting on asceticism and worship of angels,...(v.2:18)." Angels played a prominent role in their religious system serving as intermediaries between God and man. Finally, they appealed to mystical visions to authenticate their teaching - "...going on in detail about visions,...(v.2:18)." It appears that these revelations through mystical experience took precedence over Apostolic instruction. In the end, all this error did was fuel human pride and create a class of believers boasting a superior spirituality.

What we have in this loose description of the 'error' is a philosophy that includes vague echoes of Judaism (dietary laws, sabboths, and circumcision) as well as references that associate the teaching with primitive Gnosticism (ascetic practices, angel worship, and mystical experiences). Perhaps the best way to understand the Colossian error is to see it as a form of Jewish Gnosticism, or folk religion, that mixed together Jewish and primitive Gnostic ideas along with localized religious myths.

QUESTION

The pressing question is, how does the church push back against this kind of wrong teaching? This is a very relevant question, both for the church in Colossae and for us today. What Paul does is model the answer to this question in his response. He doesn't identify and counter each point of false teaching in Colossae, rather he underscores the truth of the gospel out of the conviction that a clear understanding of the truth is the best antidote for false teaching in all its forms. It's out of this conviction that the dominant themes of Colossians emerge, and these themes can be summed up in three words: Christ, church, and gospel.

As in the book of Hebrews, Paul argues for the centrality and supremacy of Christ - *"He is the image of the invisible God, the firstborn of all creation. For by him all things were created, in heaven and on earth, visible and invisible, whether thrones or dominions or rulers or authorities—all things were created through him and for him. And he is before all things, and in him all things hold together. And he is the head of the body, the church. He is the beginning, the firstborn from the dead, that in everything he might be preeminent. For in him all the fullness of God was pleased to dwell, and through him to reconcile to himself all things, whether on earth or in heaven, making peace by the blood of his cross. And you, who once were alienated and hostile in mind, doing evil deeds, he has now reconciled in his body of flesh by his death, in order to present you holy and blameless and above reproach before him (Col.1:15-22)"...."For* in him the whole fullness of deity dwells bodily, and you have been filled in him, who is the head of all rule and authority (Col.2:9,10)." Some profound things are said about Christ in these brief passages. For example, "He is the image of the invisible God;...(v.1:18)." He's God in flesh! To see Christ is to see God. Also, he plays the instrumental role in both creation and recreation, the fullness of God is embodied in him, and we're filled full in him. So, Christ alone is able to fully save those who believe, and the ascetic demands of false teachers are unnecessary. Christ is sufficient to meet all our spiritual needs. His fullness alone empowers us to live faithfully and flourish in a spiritual environment that's hostile to us.

The second word is church. In Colossians, the church is intimately connected to Christ - "...he is the head of the body, the church. He is the beginning, the firstborn from the dead, that in everything he might be preeminent (v.1:18)." The same language is used in verse 1:24 - "...for the sake of his body, that is, the church." Christ can't be separated from his redeemed people, the church, which is understood to be cosmic and universal as well as earthly and localized. Wherever the redeemed are found gathered in worship and fellowship, Christ is present. And through the activity of his

Spirit he serves, protects, and nurtures them. This being the case, it's crucial that we not diminish the importance of the earthly church's role in the believer's life. Unfortunately, this is exactly what's been done in certain Christian circles over the past years, and it's left us weaker and more vulnerable to doctrinal error.

The point that's being made by Paul with the use of this head/body metaphor is that Christ reigns, rules, works, and is made visible on earth through the life of the church. If we want to be protected from error and sustained in the faith, we must submit ourselves to the care and custody of the local church.

Finally, there's the gospel, the original 'good news', the announcement that Christ lived a sinless life, died on a cross, was buried, and raised from the dead on the third day. Because of this historical event our sins are fully forgiven! When we repent and place our trust in Christ alone for our salvation Christ's sacrifice is all that's needed; we can't contribute anything to our salvation. And yet, this gospel is often perverted through additions. It's not uncommon for false teachers to add to the gospel with 'new revelation' and religious demands, demands that compromise the integrity of grace and burden the believer with the demands of works based salvation. This is tragic because it denies the power of the cross and corrupts the gospel that promises salvation apart from moral merit, and gives us hope in the face of persistent human weakness - *"And you, who were dead in your trespasses and the uncircumcision of your flesh, God made alive together with him, having forgiven us all our trespasses, by canceling the record of debt that stood against us with its legal demands. This he set aside, nailing it to the cross. He disarmed the rulers and authorities and put them to open shame, by triumphing over them in him. Therefore let no one pass judgment on you in questions of food and drink, or* with regard to a festival or a new moon or a Sabbath. These are a shadow of the things to come, but the substance belongs to Christ (Col.2:13-17)." It's this gospel truth that caused Horatio Spafford to write these lines - "My sin, oh, the bliss of this glorious thought!

> My sin, not in part but the whole,
> Is nailed to the cross, and I bear it no more,
> Praise the Lord, praise the Lord, O my soul!"[2]

This is the power of the gospel; this is the truth!

The reality we have to face is that we're all confronted with false teaching, and our best protection against it is to fall deeply in love with Christ, stay actively involved in the life of a local church, and continue to grow in our understanding of the gospel.

2   Spafford, Horatio G., 'It Is Well With My Soul', Trinity Psalter Hymnal, (Trinity Psalter Hymnal Joint Venture, Willow Grove, PA., 2018), p. 476.

COLOSSIANS 1:1-14

"Paul, an apostle of Christ Jesus by the will of God, and Timothy our brother, To the saints and faithful brothers in Christ at Colossae: Grace to you and peace from God our Father. We always thank God, the Father of our Lord Jesus Christ, when we pray for you, since we heard of your faith in Christ Jesus and of the love that you have for all the saints, because of the hope laid up for you in heaven. Of this you have heard before in the word of the truth, the gospel, which has come to you, as indeed in the whole world it is bearing fruit and increasing—as it also does among you, since the day you heard it and understood the grace of God in truth, just as you learned it from Epaphras our beloved fellow servant. He is a faithful minister of Christ on your behalf and has made known to us your love in the Spirit. And so, from the day we heard, we have not ceased to pray for you, asking that you may be filled with the knowledge of his will in all spiritual wisdom and understanding, so as to walk in a manner worthy of the Lord, fully pleasing to him: bearing fruit in every good work and increasing in the knowledge of God; being strengthened with all power, according to his glorious might, for all endurance and patience with joy; giving thanks to the Father, who has qualified you to share in the inheritance of the saints in light. He has delivered us from the domain of darkness and transferred us to the kingdom of his beloved Son, in whom we have redemption, the forgiveness of sins."

1

Paul's Thanksgiving & Prayer

This passage is easily separated into three parts: an opening greeting (vv.1,2); a section of thanksgiving (vv.3-8); and a section of prayer (vv.9-14). The greeting is fairly standard, but the thanksgiving section is packed full of very helpful material. It's apparently been reported to Paul by Epaphras that the Christians in Colossae had expressed true faith in Christ, and that they truly loved their fellow believers - "...since we heard of your faith in Christ Jesus and of the love that you have for all the saints,...(v.4)." It appears that the majority of the believers in Colossae were remaining faithful to the gospel and were supportive of one another, and for this Paul thanks God. But the error that confronted them was persuasive and posed a real threat. Paul wants them to know that he and Timothy are praying regularly for them. However, there are two other things that will keep them strong and safe: the fact that they're 'in Christ' and that they've been instructed in the true gospel by their pastor Epaphras. There are two lines in this opening paragraph highlighting these two points - "...your faith in Christ Jesus...(v.4)" and "...the word of the truth, the gospel (v.5)." What's indicated by the phrase 'faith in Christ Jesus' is two-fold; it's saying that Christ was the object of their faith. They had placed their trust in him alone for their salvation. Also, as a result of this, their life and works of faith flow out of their union with him. They're 'in Christ Jesus'; they were living under his Lordship and care. This is where all true Christian conversion and life begins and ends. Conversion involves a spiritual condition that's changed and a life that's reordered because we've surrendered to Christ and are now living in union with him. Conversion is not simply a matter of striving to exemplify the life of Christ and do better than we did in the past; it's a deep inner work that's accomplished by the Holy Spirit; one that gives us a new heart and reorients our lives. It's God's work in us!

GOSPEL DISTINCTIVES

Directly related to this is the gospel; it also played a role in protecting the Colossians from error. There are three aspects of the gospel that distinguish it from the 'Colossian error.' First, it's true and transformative - *"...of this you have heard before in the word of the truth, the gospel, which has come to you, as indeed in the whole world it is bearing fruit and growing...(vv.5,6)."* The gospel - the good news of Christ - is objectively true and trustworthy. It has integrity because, as God's Word, it bears God's character. It stands as true in every sense of the word in contrast to the 'Colossian error' which was false. There's an inherent power in truth, and wherever the true gospel is preached lives are transformed. The gospel bears fruit! Second, the gospel is universal and timeless. In verse 6, Paul mentions that the gospel had come to the *'whole world...bearing fruit and growing.'* Unlike the 'Colossian error' that was localized in impact, the gospel captured the hearts and minds of people everywhere it was preached. Not only is the gospel universal in its appeal, it's timeless in its reach. This idea is presented to us in the use of the word 'hope' in verse 5 - *"...because of the hope laid up for you in heaven.*" This isn't 'hope' as a disposition of mind; it's not hopeful expectation. Rather, it's 'the hope' referring to the believer's inheritance, the ultimate realities, or the full expression of the redemptive promise that we'll experience in the 'Age to Come'. It speaks of the content of our inheritance and anticipates a completed salvation, a perfect righteousness, an incorruptible embodied existence, and the unbounded manifestation of eternal life. Also, this hope is oriented toward the future. It's kept securely for us in heaven. It can't be stripped away from us. And yet, it has a present influence on our lives; it inspires and energizes our faith and love - "*...since we heard of your faith in Christ Jesus and of the love that you have for all the saints, because of the hope laid up for you in heaven. Of this you have heard before in the word of the truth, the gospel,...(vv.1:4,5).*" Why the emphasis on future hope? Perhaps because the 'Colossian error' rejected the future dimension of Christian salvation and preached a time-bound gospel that was preoccupied with the present and turned its back on the life to come. This kind of Christian message is a shallow substitute for the real gospel. It satisfies only when times are good. When present circumstances turn tough and Christian faithfulness becomes more demanding, it's then that we need hope; and often it's the realities of our future inheritance that carry us through. This is why using the Bible only as a life skills manual is such a weak and short-sighted approach to discipleship. It's the rich theological understandings given to us in the Bible that strengthen our faith and broaden our spiritual horizons, so we can persevere when the harsh and demanding seasons of life come. How does the future look to you? Do you have hope beyond this life? Has your Christian understanding prepared you to die? Only the true gospel will do this.

The third and final distinguishing aspect of the gospel is that it's a message of grace - "...since the day you heard it and understood the grace of God in truth,...(v.6)." This is the radical center of the gospel: salvation is gifted to us by God's grace, not earned by our moral strivings and good works. The Colossian believers had heard and understood, and it dramatically altered their approach to religious things. It was no longer adherence to a system of ascetic disciplines - dietary laws and holy days of worship - that saved and sanctified them. Now it was salvation based on the mercy of God and the works of a Savior. This is the compelling 'good news' of the gospel! What caused Paul to give thanks to God was the work of God's grace and the gospel in the lives of the Colossian believers.

PAUL'S PRAYER

Let's consider Paul's prayer in the closing paragraph of the passage (vv.1:9-14). I want to lift a few lines from the text and string them together - "...we have not ceased to pray for you, asking that you may be filled with the knowledge of his will in all spiritual wisdom and understanding (v.9)"..."May you be strengthened with all power...for all endurance and patience with joy (v.11)"..."giving thanks to the Father, who has qualified you to share in the inheritance of the saints in light (v.12)." All the nuanced expressions of this prayer flow out of Paul's initial request that they 'be filled with the knowledge of his will... so as to walk in a manner worthy of the Lord (v.10),...." There are some general observations to be made here. One is that Paul wanted them to grow in the knowledge of God's will, not in the speculative and theoretical religious musings of the 'Colossian error.' They were to think about what was revealed, not on what remained hidden. Also, the verb 'you may be filled' is passive, indicating that we don't fill ourselves; the

Holy Spirit fills us with understanding as we give ourselves to the study of God's Word. Then 'the knowledge of his will' is an increasing understanding of what the redemptive revelation means to us who believe and also to the ultimate restoration of the Cosmos. This increasing biblical understanding is to change the way we live 'so as to walk in a manner worthy of the Lord.' Theological knowledge that doesn't change us is useless. But when growth in Christian understanding is genuine it produces a distinct way of life that speaks well of the Lord:

- A life marked by spiritual growth - "...bearing fruit in every good work and increasing in the knowledge of God (v.10)."

- A life of faithfulness - "...May you be strengthened with all power...for all endurance and patience...(v.11)."

- A life of thanksgiving - "...giving thanks to the Father,...(v.12)."

The verb translated *'always giving thanks'* is in the present tense indicating that Christian believer lives constantly in a state of thanksgiving. How can this be? The conditions of life aren't always conducive to thanksgiving. This is absolutely true, but there's something constant in the believer's life... the redemptive deliverance that we've received in Christ. This is the unchanging source of our thanksgiving - *"He has delivered us from the domain of darkness and transferred us to the kingdom of his beloved Son, in whom we have redemption, the forgiveness of sins (vv.1:13,14)."* In Christ we've experienced a profound deliverance, one that's similar yet greater than the deliverance of ethnic Israel from Egyptian bondage. We've been set free from the spiritual darkness and domination of 'sin and death.' The echoes of the Exodus are real here, but the liberation and resettlement we've received as 'spiritual Israel' is far more dramatic and substantial than that of ethnic

Israel. Our deliverance isn't temporal, it's spiritual, and our inheritance isn't 'earthbound', it's heavenly and eternal. We've been 'transferred' (translated) into the Kingdom of Christ by whom we've been bought back out of the slave market of sin by his redeeming blood. And now we stand thoroughly forgiven because of what Christ alone has done, and this redeemed standing before God never changes because it's grounded solely in the grace of God and the saving sacrifice of Christ. So we can always be thankful because God is always faithful, even though we're not.

This opening section of Colossians exposes the Apostle's heart for God's people. He wants them to grow in their understanding of their salvation and be protected by the gospel from religious error. This is the source of our safety as well. My appeal to you, as the people of God, is that you give yourselves to Christian learning and worship and find your security in what Christ alone has done on your behalf.

COLOSSIANS 1:15-23

"He is the image of the invisible God, the firstborn of all creation. For by him all things were created, in heaven and on earth, visible and invisible, whether thrones or dominions or rulers or authorities—all things were created through him and for him. And he is before all things, and in him all things hold together. And he is the head of the body, the church. He is the beginning, the firstborn from the dead, that in everything he might be preeminent. For in him all the fullness of God was pleased to dwell, and through him to reconcile to himself all things, whether on earth or in heaven, making peace by the blood of his cross. And you, who once were alienated and hostile in mind, doing evil deeds, he has now reconciled in his body of flesh by his death, in order to present you holy and blameless and above reproach before him, if indeed you continue in the faith, stable and steadfast, not shifting from the hope of the gospel that you heard, which has been proclaimed in all creation under heaven, and of which I, Paul, became a minister."

2

Christ, the Firstborn

Since we've been rescued by transference into the Kingdom of Christ, at great cost to him, we're expected to serve him with undivided devotion. This redemptive accomplishment is dramatic and wondrous, and it's grounded solely in the work of Christ at Calvary. It's appropriate, then, for us to ask the questions: who is he and why should I serve him? The passage we're considering will help us answer these questions.

EARLY HYMN OR CREEDAL FRAGMENT

It's commonly thought that verses 15-20 are an adaptation of an early Christian hymn or a creedal fragment that Paul uses to establish Christ's identity: first, in his relationship to God and the creation, and secondly, as he's related to redemption. There are two prominent stanzas that share some common language: verse 15 opens the first stanza with "He is the image of the invisible God, the firstborn of all creation", and verse 18 introduces the second stanza with "...he is the head of the body, the church. He is the beginning, the firstborn from the dead...". The shared language that exposes the central theme of each stanza is - "He is...the firstborn of all creation (v.15)" and "...he is...the firstborn from the dead (v.18)."

In these two stanzas, which are essentially creedal statements, we meet Christ as the 'Cosmic Christ', the one who reigns supreme over both the creation (Cosmos) and the re-creation (the new order established by divine redemption). The opening assertion is that in the incarnate Christ the nature and character of God is perfectly revealed - "He is (this is the nature of his being) the image (the exact representation and manifestation) of the invisible God (v.15)." Does this description sound familiar? The writer of Hebrews says something very similar - "He is the radiance of the glory of God and the exact imprint of his nature...(v.1:3)." The same idea is presented in John's gospel - "No one has ever seen God; the only God (the only begotten God, God the Son), who is at the Father's side, he has made him known (v.1:18)." When the full witness to Christ given to us in the New Testament is considered the only proper conclusion is that Christ is 'God in flesh'. He's 'God the Son', the Second Person of the Trinity, who reveals God the Father to man. This revelation is not exhaustive, but it's true and trustworthy.

In the minds of many this is a radical idea, so it has been a constant point of theological struggle. It was the basis of the Jews' accusation that Jesus was a blasphemer which then led to his crucifixion. It was also the heart of the 'Arian controversy' that led to the confessional formulation expressed in the conclusions of the Council of Nicea (4th century A.D.) -

> "We believe in one God, the Father Almighty,
> Maker of heaven and earth,
> and of all things visible and invisible.
> And in one Lord Jesus Christ, the only-begotten
> Son of God, begotten of the Father before all

Ages; God of God, Light of Light, true God of
true God; begotten, not made, being of one
substance with the Father, by whom all
things were made." (Nicene Creed, 325 A.D.)

THE FIRSTBORN

Since Christ is God, he's 'the firstborn of all creation.' This
isn't a reference to a point of beginning; Christ wasn't the
first created being. Rather, this statement establishes his
relationship to the creation. Being the 'firstborn' is to have
positional authority or the rank of ruler over the creation. He's
the 'Lord of creation' by virtue of being the 'firstborn.' There's
a Messianic statement made in Psalm 89 that helps clarify
the meaning of this 'firstborn' reference - "...I will make him
the firstborn, the highest of the Kings of the earth (v.27)." As
the 'firstborn' he'll be the ruler of Kings ('firstborn' designates
priority of rank). The New International Version renders the
Colossian verses well - "He is the image of the invisible God,
the firstborn over all creation. For in him all things were
created...(Col.1:15,16)." The point that's made in this opening
stanza is that since Christ is the instrumental means of the
entire creation, he's positioned to rule over it. And he rules
over it in its entirety, in all its dimensions: the heavenly and
the earthly; the visible and the invisible. He rules over all the
angelic hosts, and over all spiritual beings, indicated by the
reference to 'thrones', 'dominions', 'rulers', and 'authorities.'

Christ is the unifying reference point of the whole 'created
order', and this 'created order' isn't restricted to the realm of
physical reality, but also includes the spiritual dimension
of reality. The Bible presents us with this two-dimensional
understanding of what's real, which challenges the dominant
naturalistic view of our day which is a view of reality that's
stunted, superficial, and inadequate. According to Paul,

Christ stands at the beginning of the universe as its Creator, and he stands at its end, as the one to whom the cosmos brings glory. During this 'in between time' he rules and holds all things together (v.17), or as the writer of Hebrews says - "...he upholds the universe by the word of his power...(v.1:3)." What sustains the order of the Cosmos isn't an impersonal force or some dynamic idea, but a person...the resurrected Christ! It's his active presence in the universe that keeps atoms from scattering, gravity working, and the planets in their orbits. Everything in creation points to Christ as its integration point and as the cosmic ruler. For this reason, he should be obediently served.

THE COSMIC REDEEMER

If this isn't sufficient reason to serve him alone, then consider the fact that he's also the 'Cosmic redeemer.' He's the source and mediator of a redemption that is comprehensive in nature. The second stanza of the hymn states this plainly - "And he is the head of the body, the church. He is the beginning, the firstborn from the dead, that in everything he might be preeminent. For in him all the fullness of God was pleased to dwell, and through him to reconcile to himself all things, whether on earth or in heaven, making peace by the blood of his cross (vv.1:18-20)." What we have in the second stanza is Christ ,the redeemer, who brings salvation to the elect people of God and brings peace ('Shalom'-health & restoration) to the entire cosmos. Both are expressions of the reconciliation secured by Christ's death and resurrection. Since his reconciling work is exhaustive in nature, he's preeminent over all things; he exercises supreme authority over everything that exists, whether they're temporal or spiritual powers, or animate or inanimate things. This is the essential point of conflict in the ongoing divine/human struggle. Who's going to be in charge, God or I? This is the essence of the original sin: Adam wanted to be like God, he wanted to be in charge. He wanted to determine for himself what was good and what was evil.

What ultimately positions Christ to be the cosmic redeemer and peace-maker is the fact that he's God - "For in him all the fullness of God was pleased to dwell (v.1:19)." Only God can redeem a people for himself through death and resurrection because he alone has life in himself. Notice what he's done redemptively - "He is the beginning, the firstborn from the dead,...(v.19)." The idea is that Christ is the beginning of something because he's the first to conquer death in resurrection. In this context, 'firstborn' refers to temporal priority; Christ is the first of many to follow. He's the 'beginning', or founder, of a new kind of humanity - the redeemed - who will also experience bodily resurrection at his return (1Cor.15). In this way he's the 'firstborn among many brothers' (Rom.8:29). As Redeemer, Christ has become the head of a new kind of man, a people reconciled to God and restored to their true humanity.

Also, the impact of the death and resurrection of Christ is comprehensive - "and through him to reconcile to himself all things, whether on earth or in heaven, making peace by the blood of his cross (v.20)." The unspoken understanding is that the harmony of the cosmos has suffered disruption and is in a state of 'futility' (Rom.8:20-23). It's held in bondage to corruption and groans for liberation and renewal. This liberation has come through the cross of Christ! Because of Calvary, the entire Creation will be brought back under the rule of the 'Cosmic Christ' and God will be 'all in all' (1Cor.15:28). This is not suggesting a universal salvation; it's referring to a universal restoration under the Lordship of Christ. In this hymn, or creedal fragment, we're confronted with the 'Cosmic Christ' who is preeminent, supreme, and transcendent. He is worthy of our loyal devotion!

PERSONALIZING THE TRANSCENDENT

Paul doesn't leave the discussion in this cosmic context, impersonal and somewhat abstract and other worldly. Instead he closes this section by personalizing the transcendent work of Christ - *"And you, who once were alienated and hostile in mind, doing evil deeds, he has now reconciled in his body of flesh by his death, in order to present you holy and blameless and above reproach before him, if indeed you continue in the faith, stable and steadfast, not shifting from the hope of the gospel that you heard, which has been proclaimed in all creation under heaven, and of which I, Paul, became a minister (vv.1:21-23)."* In this paragraph there's an abrupt shift in perspective from the cosmic to the personal. The opening address is emphatic..."And you." And you Colossian believers, who were once spiritually dead, separated and hostile to God in thoughts and deeds; you've been reconciled to God through the saving work of Christ in history...'in his body of flesh by his death'. The work of salvation wasn't a cosmic abstraction, it was a real flesh and blood physical sacrifice and death that saved you. For this reason, continue to serve him. Don't deviate from trusting Christ alone for your salvation, and rest securely in the fact that you'll be presented before Christ at his coming, holy, declared blameless, and free from any condemning accusations. All our spiritual needs are met fully in Christ; so don't look anywhere else, but serve him only and serve him passionately!

The profound 'good news' of the gospel is that the 'Cosmic Christ' is a personal Savior. And because of his saving work we've been delivered from the 'dominion of darkness' and brought into the freedom of his rule.

COLOSSIANS 1:24-2:5

"Now I rejoice in my sufferings for your sake, and in my flesh I am filling up what is lacking in Christ's afflictions for the sake of his body, that is, the church, of which I became a minister according to the stewardship from God that was given to me for you, to make the word of God fully known, the mystery hidden for ages and generations but now revealed to his saints. To them God chose to make known how great among the Gentiles are the riches of the glory of this mystery, which is Christ in you, the hope of glory. Him we proclaim, warning everyone and teaching everyone with all wisdom, that we may present everyone mature in Christ. For this I toil, struggling with all his energy that he powerfully works within me. For I want you to know how great a struggle I have for you and for those at Laodicea and for all who have not seen me face to face, that their hearts may be encouraged, being knit together in love, to reach all the riches of full assurance of understanding and the knowledge of God's mystery, which is Christ, in whom are hidden all the treasures of wisdom and knowledge. I say this in order that no one may delude you with plausible arguments. For though I am absent in body, yet I am with you in spirit, rejoicing to see your good order and the firmness of your faith in Christ."

3

Paul: a Minister

Paul is a minister of the gospel and the first thing he associates with this calling is suffering, and there are several things that distinguish his suffering and make it unique. One is that it was Apostolic. Paul was an Apostle of the first order. His ministry was groundbreaking and foundational for the church. It was a uniquely demanding ministry that was discharged at the cost of persecution and great personal sacrifice. Also, Paul's suffering benefited the church for all time - *"...I rejoice in my sufferings for your sake (the Colossian Christians) ...for the sake of his body, that is, the church (a more open reference)."* Paul's sufferings were purposeful: they contributed to the establishment of the church and the forming of the church's theological voice. Then, Paul's suffering was an extension of the sufferings of Christ - *"...in my flesh I am filling up what is lacking in Christ's afflictions... (v.24)."* The Apostle isn't suggesting that the redemptive sufferings of Christ were insufficient or incomplete and needed to be completed by him. Rather, the ministry of the Apostles was an extension of the ministry of Christ; they were his Ambassadors. To persecute them was to persecute Christ. The resistance and persecution that accompanied Christ's ministry accompanied the Apostles' ministry as well. This wasn't unexpected, the disciples had been forewarned

- *"If the world hates you, know that it has hated me before it hated you....A servant is not greater than his master. If they persecuted me, they will also persecute you (Jn. 15:18, 20)."*

PROPHETIC WORD FULFILLED

This prophetic word was fulfilled in all the Apostles' lives. For Paul, suffering was part of his missionary and pastoral work, and also, part of his prison experience. And yet, God was always at work in the midst of his afflictions. Aware of this, Paul rejoiced in suffering because he understood that the outcome of his suffering was beneficial to the church. Not only benefitting the first century church, but also us, 21st century believers, who are still receiving instruction, correction, and encouragement from the inspired writings of Paul. In addition to this, the Apostolic ministry of Paul was characterized by striving (toil, struggle, spiritual labor) - *"For this I toil, struggling with all his energy that he powerfully works within me. For I want you to know how great a struggle I have for you and for those at Laodicea and for all who have not seen me face to face (Col. 1:29-2:1)."* Paul was engaged in the hard work of Christian ministry in an effort to preserve the integrity of the gospel and stimulate the spiritual well being of the church. This involved striving and contending for the faith. Contending is a particular kind of struggle. It's the struggle associated with preaching and protecting the gospel against the distortions of false teachers. It's the labor of admonishing and instructing Christian converts.

For Paul there were two fundamental factors that made him effective and kept him engaged in the struggle. One was that he saw himself as a servant of the gospel, a man enslaved to the Word of God - "Of this gospel I was made a minister/servant....(Eph. 3:7)." The second factor was that he was aware that in his own strength he wasn't able to engage the task -

"Such is the confidence that we have through Christ toward God. Not that we are sufficient in ourselves to claim anything as coming from us, but our sufficiency is from God, who has made us sufficient to be ministers of a new covenant...(2 Cor. 3:4-6)." In verse 29 of our text Paul writes something similar - *"For this I toil, struggling with all his energy that he powerfully works within me."* What Paul wants understood is that the struggles of gospel ministry and the demands of Christian life can only be engaged faithfully through the enabling grace of God and the energizing presence of the Holy Spirit in our lives. For Paul the Apostolic call was a call to struggle, toil, and the strivings of servanthood. In many ways this is the nature of ordinary Christian life as well. The demands of Christian faithfulness are beyond our ability to fulfill. It's only as we acknowledge our weakness, surrender to Christ, and rely on the empowering of the Holy Spirit that we'll experience any degree of faithfulness to Christ and his call.

Apostolic ministry, for Paul, was defined by suffering and striving; and finally, it's a ministry of proclamation. As an Apostle, he was called to proclaim the good news of Christ. This was certainly Paul's preoccupation, he was a passionate preacher of Christ - *"of which I became a minister according to the stewardship from God that was given to me for you, to make the word of God fully known, the mystery hidden for ages and generations but now revealed to his saints. To them God chose to make known how great among the Gentiles are the riches of the glory of this mystery, which is Christ in you, the hope of glory. Him we proclaim, warning everyone and teaching everyone with all wisdom, that we may present everyone mature in Christ."....."* that their hearts may be encouraged, being knit together in love, to reach all the riches of full assurance of understanding and the knowledge of God's mystery, which is Christ, in whom are hidden all the* *treasures of wisdom and knowledge (Col.1:25-28; 2:2,3)."* The most concise statement of what Paul was called to proclaim is found in verse 28 (ch.1) - "Him we proclaim..." Gospel proclamation is the preaching of Christ, telling his story and exploring the redemptive implications of his life, death, and resurrection. Paul states this conviction when he writes to the Corinthians - "For I decided to know nothing among you except Jesus Christ and him crucified (1Cor.2:2)." Christ is the heart of the gospel and the focus of gospel proclamation.

THREE ADDITIONAL FEATURES

Without diminishing this 'core' of the gospel Paul identifies additional features of Apostolic preaching. There are three to which I want to draw your attention: first, Apostolic preaching was an inclusive proclamation. It's the "mystery...revealed to his saints (Col.1:26)." Saints being all those set apart to God through Christ, and these include Gentiles (v.1:27). Paul preached Christ to everyone without discrimination. He preached to Jews and Gentiles, men and women, rich and poor, as well as to the educated and illiterate. The gospel is to be preached to all people everywhere, not to a spiritual elite only as the false teachers taught. Secondly, Apostolic preaching is the proclamation of a mystery, something once hidden but is now revealed. Writing to the Corinthians, Paul writes - "This is how one should regard us (Apostles) , as servants of Christ and stewards of the mysteries of God (1Cor.4:1)." The Christian mystery is disclosed throughout the New Testament in varied nuanced ways, and yet it's a mystery that is always grounded in Christ. In the case of Colossians, it's the mystery of "Christ in you, the hope of glory (v.1:27)." The 'good news' is that as Christian believers we're indwelt with the abiding presence of Christ through the infilling of the Holy Spirit. Not only are we 'in Christ', but he's 'in us.' So the new life we have in Christ is a life empowered and animated by Christ 'in us'. This same idea is echoed in Paul's statement to the Galatians - *"I have been crucified with Christ. It is no longer I who live, but Christ who lives in me. And the life I now live in the flesh I live by faith in the Son of God, who loved me and gave himself for me (v.2:20)."* The point is: it's the power and grace of Christ that saves us, and it's the power and grace of Christ that sanctifies and sustains us. Lastly, Apostolic preaching is the proclamation that gives us assurance of future glory. The mystery is - "Christ in you, the hope of glory (v.1:27)." Christ in us now gives us the 'hope'/'certainty' that we'll share in his glory on the day of resurrection; the day when the 'children of God' will be revealed - *"For I consider that the sufferings of this present time are not worth comparing with the glory that is to be revealed to us. For the creation waits with eager longing for the revealing of the sons of God. For the creation was subjected to futility, not willingly, but because of him who subjected it, in hope that the creation itself will be set free from its bondage to corruption and obtain the freedom of the glory of the children of God. For we know that the whole creation has been groaning together in the pains of childbirth until now. And not only the creation, but we ourselves, who have the firstfruits of the Spirit, groan inwardly as we wait eagerly for adoption as sons, the redemption of our bodies. For in this hope we were saved....(Rom.8:18-24)."* The mystery of the gospel - Christ in us - gives us the sure assurance that we have a heavenly inheritance which is eternal life, an embodied existence in a restored cosmos free from sin and death. This is real hope! Do you have it?

This passage should fill us with gratitude and thanksgiving because we've inherited the sure hope of the gospel through the suffering and faithful proclamation of Christ by others. Let's commit ourselves fully to Christ and determine that we'll be faithful followers as well.

COLOSSIANS 2:6-15

"Therefore, as you received Christ Jesus the Lord, so walk in him, rooted and built up in him and established in the faith, just as you were taught, abounding in thanksgiving. See to it that no one takes you captive by philosophy and empty deceit, according to human tradition, according to the elemental spirits of the world, and not according to Christ. For in him the whole fullness of deity dwells bodily, and you have been filled in him, who is the head of all rule and authority. In him also you were circumcised with a circumcision made without hands, by putting off the body of the flesh, by the circumcision of Christ, having been buried with him in baptism, in which you were also raised with him through faith in the powerful working of God, who raised him from the dead. And you, who were dead in your trespasses and the uncircumcision of your flesh, God made alive together with him, having forgiven us all our trespasses, by canceling the record of debt that stood against us with its legal demands. This he set aside, nailing it to the cross. He disarmed the rulers and authorities and put them to open shame, by triumphing over them in him."

4

Let No One Take You Captive

This section of chapter 2 (vv.6-15) forms the theological heart of the book of Colossians. It contains Paul's essential points of argument against the false teaching that was threatening the integrity of the gospel as already preached in Colossae by Epaphras, their faithful Pastor. Paul has already identified himself as a minister of the gospel struggling to faithfully proclaim the good news of Christ. He expresses great concern for the Colossian Christians even though he had never met them personally. They were, in fact, his spiritual grandchildren because they had come to Christ under the ministry of Epaphras who had been converted in Ephesus under the ministry of Paul. One thing that Paul's concern exposes is his keen sense of responsibility for new believers; he wanted to make sure that they were properly instructed and protected. So he responded quickly to the news that false teachers had come to Colossae and were calling into question the sufficiency of Christ's saving work and diminishing Christ's exclusive role in redemptive history. They weren't necessarily taking away from the gospel but they were adding to it by teaching that religious works had to be added to the work of Christ if one's salvation was to be secure and spiritual 'fullness' was to be acquired. The saving sacrifice of Christ wasn't enough on its own.

This passage comprises two paragraphs, one short (vv.6,7) and the other more substantial (vv.8-15). The first paragraph summaries Paul's expectation of the reader's response to his earlier prayer and admonition (1:9-12; 2:4,5). In light of this prayer and earlier admonition Paul makes his initial appeal - *"....as you received Christ Jesus the Lord, so walk in him,...(v.6)."* Since you've confessed Christ's Lordship over your life and embraced the Apostolic teaching about him, 'continue to live your life in him.' Let Christ establish your values, renew your thinking, and determine your conduct. This 'living in him' is shaped by being 'rooted and built up in him' and by being 'established in the faith' (v.7). Being 'rooted and built up in him' stresses the understanding that Christian growth is dependent on our being bound up in Christ. Spiritual formation in the believer's life is the result of being in a dynamic Spirit-enlivened relationship with Christ. An arid intellectualism will never produce vibrant Christian virtues. Christian growth involves both the transformation of mind and heart. We're also to be 'built up in him.' Paul wanted them to build on their understanding of Christ's person and work. If our understanding of who Christ is and what he's done is wrong, then the whole structure of our Christian lives will be skewed and misdirected.

IN THE FAITH

Paul, then, wanted them to be 'established in the faith.' When the Apostle uses the phrase, 'in the faith', he's referring to a body of teaching or the doctrinal content of Christian belief. The key to understanding how this establishment in the faith occurs is found in the tense and mood of the verb 'established.' The verb is a present passive indicating that God by his Word and Spirit does the establishing over time. We'll never become grounded in the faith so that we're able to withstand the pressures and appeals of false teaching apart from consistent exposure to biblical instruction over time. 'Establishing' is a process, and it's completely dependent on the preached Word and the quickening of the Holy Spirit. We need to be established in the faith, so we need to regularly present ourselves to God in worship and by the disciplined hearing of his Word. Question: are you committed to growing in the faith? If you are, it will be reflected in the priorities and worship patterns of your life.

The second paragraph of the passage is a warning that leads to a theological explanation of why the Colossian believers should reject the false teaching they were confronted with - *"See to it that no one takes you captive by philosophy and empty deceit, according to human tradition, according to the elemental spirits of the world, and not according to Christ (v.2:8)."* The warning is quite straightforward...don't be taken captive or carried off by forms of teaching that are alien to the gospel. According to Paul these foreign ideas are expressions of empty and deceptive philosophy. This isn't a generalized condemnation of philosophical inquiry, but a specific warning related to the false teachers in Colossae. Their teaching was empty and devoid of intellectual, moral, and spiritual value as well as deceptive. It appealed to their intellectual pride and led to false assurance. This 'philosophy' stood in apposition to the true gospel; it was deceptive whereas the gospel is true and spiritually transformative.

DECEPTION

There were reasons why this false teaching was so deceptive. First, it was the product of human 'tradition', not divine revelation (v.8). Also, it was 'according to the elemental spirits of the world' (v.8). This is an ambiguous and much debated line of text, but a sensible understanding is that it was philosophy shaped by the prevailing religious speculations of the day that gave spiritual significance to material things and ascetic practices that ultimately led to works based religion (v.2:16). However, the great failing of this false teaching was that it wasn't 'according to Christ.' It promoted ideas that undermined total dependence on Christ by challenging the Apostolic teaching that emphasized the sufficiency of Christ; the fact that embodied in Jesus is the final revelation of God to man, and the conviction that human redemption and spiritual 'fullness' is provided only in him. Any teaching that diminishes the significance of Christ should be considered with much suspicion.

In the remaining verses of this passage (vv.9-15) Paul exposes the wrongness of the false teachers' teaching by clarifying a right understanding of Christ and what is provided in him. There are two fundamental understandings: first, Christ is God - *"...in him the whole fullness of deity dwells bodily (v.9)"*; secondly, as Christian believers we're complete in him - *"...you have been filled (filled full) in him,... (v.10)."* The first affirmation that in Christ 'the whole fullness of deity dwells bodily' establishes two distinct Christian understandings. One is that Christ is fully God, he embodied 'the whole fullness of deity.' To see Jesus is to see God. The companion to this understanding is that Christ is fully God 'in flesh' - *"...in him the whole fullness of deity dwells bodily".* This idea of incarnation countered the common understanding of that day that true spiritual fullness could only be achieved by abandoning or subduing the body. This led to a disdain for physical things and the rigorous discipline of the body through ascetic practices. But the gospel announces that spiritual fullness is actually gifted to us through the bodily existence, death, and resurrection of Christ. We are embodied beings, and physical things are good, but broken. The redemption provided in Christ will restore us physically as well as spiritually.

It's out of the divine fullness of Christ that we're filled when we place our faith in him. Our spiritual needs are fully met in Christ, so additional religious strivings aren't needed. Ascetic practices and mystical experiences aren't required to achieve spiritual fullness or a deeper spiritual life. God has decisively revealed himself in Christ; nothing then in addition to our relationship with him is needed for us to know and experience the fullness of God.

DEFINING FEATURES

Looking more closely at the spiritual fullness we've received in Christ, it's distinguished by three defining features: spiritual circumcision, spiritual quickening, and spiritual liberation. Verse 11 is an interesting and challenging line of text - *"In him also you were circumcised with a circumcision made without hands...by (by virtue of) the circumcision of Christ..."* By being in union with Christ through true conversion we've been circumcised in heart and set apart to God to live a new kind of life. In this context, circumcision speaks of Christian conversion and Christ is viewed as a corporate figure, so as the whole of humanity is gathered up in Adam and died in him, the 'elect' are gathered up in the 'circumcision of Christ', which is his atoning sacrifice. From God's perspective, we were with Christ in his death, burial, and resurrection. At Calvary we died to the dictates and domination of our sinful nature, in that we were legally released from any obligation to our sin nature and were empowered by the Holy Spirit to live Christ-honoring lives. By being 'in Christ' through true conversion and by positionally participating in Christ's circumcision (the Cross) we're no longer held captive to sin, death, and the flesh; rather, we're now governed by righteousness, life, grace, and the Holy Spirit. The point Paul's making is that the sinful impulses of the flesh aren't conquered by human disciplines or ascetic rule keeping; they're defeated by the spiritual fullness gifted to us in Christ. Jesus is enough!

Notice the reference to water baptism in verse 12 - *"... having been buried with him in baptism, in which you were also raised with him through faith in the powerful working of God, who raised him from the dead."* Here baptism serves both as a sign of the New Covenant promise and as a shorthand reference to Christian conversion which is grounded in regeneration, faith, and repentance. This 'baptism', or 'circumcision of heart' (conversion), quickens us spiritually and gives us new life - *"And you, who were dead in your trespasses and the uncircumcision of your flesh, God made alive together with him, having forgiven us all our trespasses, by canceling the record of debt that stood against us with its legal demands. This he set aside, nailing it to the cross (vv.13,14)."* What's important to see here is that this spiritual quickening is inseparably tied to forgiveness of sins and the work of the Cross. When we come to Christ in repentance and faith we are thoroughly forgiven, all of our sins are covered. Additionally, the 'record of debt' that condemned us is canceled. All of us signed an IOU, promising God perfect obedience (a covenant of works) and we've all failed to keep it (Rom.3:23). This is the basis of our condemnation. But at Calvary Christ canceled the debt by taking our judgment; the IOU was torn up. The 'covenant of condemnation' no longer has power over us because we died to it 'in Christ' and we've fulfilled its demands through the perfect obedience of Christ. What flows out of this new standing in Christ is a new kind of life that reflects the character and perfections of Jesus.

LIBERATION

Finally, it's 'in Christ' that we receive spiritual liberation - *"He disarmed the rulers and authorities (the demonic powers) and put them to open shame, by triumphing over them in him (v.15)."* Here Paul makes it plain that the demonic has been stripped of its power at Calvary, and this reality was publicly displayed in the resurrection and ascension of Christ. It's to be understood that these demonic forces aren't completely destroyed, but their power is restrained and they can't harm those who live under the Lordship of Christ.

What Paul wants to impress on us is that Christ alone is sufficient to save, sustain, and sanctify his people. The 'fullness of deity' is embodied in Christ and because of this we receive spiritual fullness in him. In him we're fully saved, we're fully enlivened, and we're fully free. The gospel is the message of Christ plus nothing, and wherever it's faithfully preached our attention is lifted to him and him alone.

COLOSSIANS 2:16-23

"Therefore let no one pass judgment on you in questions of food and drink, or with regard to a festival or a new moon or a Sabbath. These are a shadow of the things to come, but the substance belongs to Christ. Let no one disqualify you, insisting on asceticism and worship of angels, going on in detail about visions, puffed up without reason by his sensuous mind, and not holding fast to the Head, from whom the whole body, nourished and knit together through its joints and ligaments, grows with a growth that is from God. If with Christ you died to the elemental spirits of the world, why, as if you were still alive in the world, do you submit to regulations— "Do not handle, Do not taste, Do not touch" (referring to things that all perish as they are used)—according to human precepts and teachings? These have indeed an appearance of wisdom in promoting self-made religion and asceticism and severity to the body, but they are of no value in stopping the indulgence of the flesh."

5

Let No One Disqualify You

This passage gives us the only explicit information about the false teaching confronting the Colossian Christians. What Paul does here is elaborate on the admonition he gave in verse 8. In fact, the structural similarities between verse 8 and verses 18 and 19 are quite apparent - *"See to it that no one takes you captive by philosophy and empty deceit, according to human tradition, according to the elemental spirits of the world, and not according to Christ (v.8)"....."Let no one disqualify you, insisting on asceticism and worship of angels, going on in detail about visions, puffed up without reason by his sensuous mind, and not holding fast to the Head, from whom the whole body, nourished and knit together through its joints and ligaments, grows with a growth that is from God (vv.18,19)."* The most important point to keep in mind is that the fatal flaw in the false teacher's teaching was that it diverted attention away from Christ and the sufficiency of his saving work. In verse 8 the language is clear; the teaching of the false teachers was *"...not according to Christ"*, and in verse 19 the same thing is stated using metaphor - *"...not holding fast to the Head (Christ)."* Rather than being the product of divine revelation, this aberrant teaching was rooted in 'human tradition', in the precepts and teaching of mere men, and was shaped by 'the elemental spirits of the world.' This reference to 'elemental spirits' is obscure and troubling. They taught principles that were sourced in the demonic. What makes the broader theme of Colossians, which is the sufficiency of Christ, relevant to us is that the recurring challenge to the gospel is: is Christ alone sufficient to save, sustain, and sanctify his people? Paul's answer is a resounding 'yes'! What Paul has done in the previous paragraph (vv.9-15) is establish the theological basis for his conviction, and now he applies his theological understanding to the Colossian situation.

The 'therefore' that opens verse 16 transitions Paul's thinking from the theological to the applicational. This application of theology to the practical concerns of church life is what keeps the church healthy and strong. The conjunctive adverb, 'therefore', in verse 16 reaches back to Paul's theology of fullness, and on the basis of this theological understanding Paul exhorts the Colossian Christians to resist the teaching of the false teachers. The fact is that the fullness of deity is embodied in Christ (v.9) and we who have come to faith in Christ are spiritually complete in him (v.10). In other words, the redemptive grace provided to those who are trusting Christ alone for salvation is not lacking in any way. The additional works that were being called for by the false teachers were incompatible with the gospel. We need to be careful when confronted with a gospel that doesn't encourage confidence in the finished work of Christ, but makes additional religious and moral demands in order to merit salvation and achieve sanctification.

Again, Paul's appeal - *"...let no one pass judgment on you in questions of food and drink, or with regard to a festival or a new moon or a Sabbath (v.16)."* The judgment was that placing confidence in the sufficiency of Christ's saving work alone was deficient; moral works and ascetic practices needed to be added to it. It was a 'Christ plus works' gospel which is not gospel at all. Paul's response is this: don't let anyone make this kind of judgment or even suggest that Christ isn't enough, because accepting this judgment leads to spiritual captivity and redemptive disqualification (vv.8,18). It leads to constant religious strivings and endless failure. If Christ's atoning death and resurrection isn't enough we'll never be saved!

ADDITIONAL DEMANDS

Notice the nature of the additional demands being made by the false teachers, they reflect both Jewish and primitive Gnostic influences. According to verse 16 there were dietary restrictions, festival and holy day celebrations, and rigorous Sabbath keeping; all reflecting Jewish tradition. Paul reminds them that these practices are only *"...a shadow of the good things to come, but the substance belongs to Christ (v.17)."* Because of this, these practices have no merit, Christ has come, the Age of promise is over, and the Age of fulfillment and fullness has arrived. Mixed in with these Jewish influences were a broad array of pagan practices: asceticism, self-abasement, worship of angels, and boasting about visions and mystical experiences. Perhaps, these ascetic practices were promoted as spiritual techniques used to prepare worshipers to receive visions and mystical experiences. But all this mystical orientation accomplished was to fuel pride and attitudes of superiority making them judgmental and exposing their lack of true spirituality. This is the predictable result of all forms of natural religion; it only produces pride masquerading as humility. It's self-deception. It's unspiritual minds oriented toward the world rather than Christ. This was the fatal failing in the false teacher's teaching. It wasn't *'holding fast to the Head* (v.19)', it wasn't *'according to Christ* (v.18)'. In their preoccupation with ascetic rules, spiritual beings, and visions, they lost confidence in Christ, who is the only sure source of true spiritual flourishing. They turned away from total dependance on Christ and asserted prideful reliance on self driven works. This is a great mistake! The 'head'/'body' metaphor that's used here (v.19) indicates that the 'Head' animates and directs the body; there is no real spiritual growth and Christian development apart from Christ. It's from him that *"...the whole body is nourished and knit together..."* and *"...grows with a growth that is from God."*

There is a distinct shift in mood beginning with verse 20. Paul has been making strong appeals in the form of imperative statements - *"...let no one pass judgment on you...(v.16)"..."Let no one disqualify you,...(v.18)."* Now he uses an indicative to make a strong statement of fact which clarifies why they've been freed from religious rule-keeping as a means to merit salvation - *"If (since) with Christ you died to the elemental spirits of the world, why, as if you were still alive in the world, do you submit to regulations -(v.20)."* The true nature of their standing in Christ rendered the demands of the false teachers foolish and useless. Because of the biblical idea of corporate solidarity, Paul claims that we who have come to Christ have died with him and now enjoy the benefits of Christ's death because we're in union with him. The fundamental benefit is *"...you died to the elemental spirits of the world..."*. The verb, 'died to', speaks of legal severance and the freedom that follows it. A good paraphrase is: *"you have died with Christ (a statement of fact) and he has set you free from the evil powers of this world (legal consequence)."* An example of corporate solidarity was the Union's conscription statute during the Civil War that allowed you to pay someone to serve in your place and satisfy your military obligation. If the person serving your term was killed, you died with him because he was serving in your place. If there was a subsequent attempt to draft you, you could say, "I've already died in this war, you can't touch me."

This would stand up in any court in the Union. Christians are freed from any legal obligation to the demonic forces in the world, and from any ascetic demands designed to appease these forces. The world is no longer our true home and no longer dictates who we are and how we should live. So Paul says, don't surrender to the demands of these false teachers because they're of the world and absolutely insensitive to the glorious benefits of being 'in Christ.'

REJECTION

What the Apostle does in verse 21 is expose the nature of the false teachers' regulations. There's a tone of sarcasm here - *"Do not handle, Do not taste, Do not touch."* 'Do not taste' refers to abstinence from certain foods and drinks. 'Handle not' and 'touch not' are probably two ways of mocking the false teachers' attitude toward the physical world. Paul's being dismissive of these disciplines as a means to live in harmony with the 'elemental spirits' or spiritual forces in the world. The reasons for his rejection of these practices is that they're temporal and human in origin (v.22), and merely impotent appearances incapable of contributing to spiritual transformation (v.23). *The New International Version* renders the verse well - *"Such regulations indeed have an appearance of wisdom, with their self-imposed worship, their false humility and their harsh treatment of the body, but they lack any value in restraining sensual indulgence."* This is Paul's conclusion: the teaching of the false teachers was deceptive and superficial, and only had an appearance of wisdom. In actuality it couldn't deliver on what it promised. Their philosophy consisted of 'will worship' that promoted asceticism and abuse of the body. It was a perversion of the gospel designed to give an impression of humility and deep spirituality when, in fact, it was spiritually superficial and powerless.

TRUE SALVATION

Where, then, do we turn to find true salvation, assurance, and transformation? We turn to Christ and the true gospel. It's 'in Christ' that we're declared righteous before God, and our lives are transformed through the struggles of faith. It's 'in Christ' that we'll ultimately be glorified and changed into incorruptible beings. Paul's conviction is that only a changed mind and heart leads to true holiness. Christian virtues aren't put on as ornamental dress; rather, developing Christian character confirms growth in Christ and the transforming nature of Christian conversion. The impulses of the sin nature can't be conquered through rigorous rule-keeping; they can only be restrained. The only sure way to achieve substantial transformation of character and life is through total dependence on Christ, believing that if we're in union with him we're a 'new creation' (2Cor.5:17).

Loving Christ more and knowing Christ better is the key to *"...stopping the indulgence of the flesh (v.23)."* A portion of C. H. Spurgeon's pastoral prayer prayed on October 12, 1879 makes this point well - "O Savior, make us like Thyself; we wish not so much to do, as to be. If Thou wilt make us to be right, we shall do right. We have often to put a constraint upon ourselves to be right; but oh, that we were like Thee, Jesus, so that we had but to act out ourselves to act out perfect holiness. We shall never rest till this is the case, till Thou hast made us to be inwardly holy; and then words and actions must be holy as a matter of course."[1]

---

1   Spurgeon, C. H., *The Pastor in Prayer*, (Emerald House Group Inc., Leeds, England, 1997), p. 86.

COLOSSIANS 3:1-4

"If then you have been raised with Christ, seek the things that are above, where Christ is, seated at the right hand of God. 2 Set your minds on things that are above, not on things that are on earth. 3 For you have died, and your life is hidden with Christ in God. When Christ who is your life appears, then you also will appear with him in glory."

6

Appearing in Glory

The theme verse of the book of Colossians is verse 6 of chapter 2 - *"Therefore, as you received Christ Jesus the Lord, so walk in him,...."* What verses 1-4 of chapter 3 do is introduce the moral implications of being a Christian believer, and transition the reader from theological considerations to the ethical expectations of those who are truly converted. There is a connection made that the Apostle Paul typically makes: Christian belief reshapes human behavior. He's saying to the Colossians, and also to us, that since you've acknowledged Christ as Lord and are now in union with him - "walk - or live - in him." The admonition is that we should live lives that reflect well on Christ, the Lord we now serve.

There are two strong appeals made in the opening four verses of Colossians 3 that form the dominant theme - *"...seek the things that are above...*(v.1)" and "Set your minds on the things *that are above...*(v.2)." What needs to be underscored is the theological grounding point for these appeals. It's stated in the opening line of verse 1 - *"If [since] then you have been raised with Christ, seek the things that are above, where Christ is,...."* Since we've been quickened and brought to life, spiritually, through union with Christ, our affections and orientation of mind are to be set on the values and virtues of the kingdom Christ rules. The moral vision called for by Christ is to be 'fleshed out' in our lives. This is an extraordinary understanding; Paul is saying that since we've been sovereignly regenerated by an act of God's grace we've been brought into a relationship with Christ that is so intimate that we can say, 'we died with Christ and we've been raised with Christ to new life.' When we place our faith in Christ alone for our salvation, we immediately pass from a state of spiritual death into a condition of spiritual life. So, setting our minds on the 'things above' is a necessary consequence of true Christian conversion. And it's necessary because the 'things above', or the heavenly values and virtues, are the furnishings of our native home. They are more compatible with our new nature and the expected fruit of the Holy Spirit's work.

THINK MORE DEEPLY

We need to think more deeply about this. Seeking the things that are above and setting our minds on things above isn't simply becoming heavenly minded, nor is it purely an intellectual exercise; rather, it's an orientation of mind and will that's always present. The verb translated 'set your minds on' is a present imperative. It's a strong appeal to develop a habit of mind and will that has a Godward focus, rather than being preoccupied with earthly things. Paul's calling us away from worldliness which is an approach to living that appeals to pride and self-promotion. He's saying that if we're truly converted our orientation of mind and will will be heavenward. We'll have a desire to pursue the things of God and live in a way that pleases him. This conviction is very much a part of Paul's thinking. Consider this passage from Philippians chapter 3 - *"Not that I have already obtained this or am already perfect, but I press on to make it my own, because Christ Jesus has made me his own. Brothers, I do not consider that I have made it my own. But one thing I do: forgetting what lies behind and straining forward to what lies ahead, I press on toward the goal for the prize of the upward call of God in Christ Jesus (vv.12-14)."* As followers of Christ our ambition should be to take possession of and live out the traits of character and the way of life that Christ has called us to. This will reorder every area of our lives: our priorities, our moral sensibilities, matters of stewardship, and our spiritual longings. Our habits of mind and will are crucial to this reorientation because they inevitably shape who we are and how we live. This heavenward orientation is expected to come to us quite naturally because that's where Christ is 'seated at the right hand of God', forever exalted to a position of honor, authority, and supremacy. For the truly converted it's an instinctive orientation, and yet it's not embraced without spiritual struggle. We must assert our wills in this Godward direction and 'seek - strive to lay hold of - the things that are above'. And we desire this because Christ is our Lord, and a servant's attention and loyalty is always drawn to his master.

Paul strengthens his appeal in verses 3 & 4 by saying that our reorientation of mind and will is the result of being repositioned in Christ which causes us to be forward looking and hopeful - *"For you have died and your life is hidden with Christ in God. When Christ who is your life appears, then you also will appear with him in glory."* The last line of verse 3 is a curious description of our present state, we're 'hidden with Christ in God'. In one sense it's telling us that we're held secure and safe in Christ. We're being protected and preserved by the same grace that saves us. So, we can be confident that the redemptive work begun in us will be completed. However, there's another sense in which this line can be understood that fits better contextually, and that is that the true and glorious nature of our redeemed state is hidden, it's veiled and presently not fully disclosed, but it will be! This is the point that's made in verse 4 where the verb 'appear' serves as the counterpoint to the verb 'hidden' in verse 3. As Christian believers our lives and destinies are legally and organically bound up in Christ, so when he died, we died, and when he was raised from the dead, we were raised as well. As a result, our bodily resurrection is guaranteed, and when he appears at his return we'll appear with him.

APPEARING IN GLORY

What distinguishes this event is that we'll 'appear with him in glory'. What we need to understand is that this isn't referring to a location, but rather to a condition. We'll appear in a glorified state. When Christ returns, the veiled nature of his incarnation will be laid aside and he'll present himself in the full weight and splendor of his divine perfections, and we'll appear with him: glorified, substantial, and fully human. No longer shadowy creatures perverted by our sinfulness, but fully freed from our struggle with sin and the flesh, completely liberated from our fallen nature. We'll be solid creatures displaying human perfections as God intended. This is what Paul refers to earlier in the book as 'the hope of glory' (Col.1:27). John, the Apostle, states it very simply - *"Beloved, we are God's children now, and what we will be has not yet appeared; but we know that when he appears we shall be like him - like the embodied Son of God - because we shall see him as he is (1Jn.3:2)."*

We'll not become little gods or angels, but we'll become perfect man, expressing a perfect humanity in incorruptible and immortal bodies. In 1 Corinthians 15 Paul refers to this 'glorified' body as a 'spiritual body'; a physical body that's compatible with a sinless Holy Spirit-dominated environment - a body that's designed and fit for eternity. Is this just wishful thinking, or is it a prominent expectation in the New Testament? It's prominent, it's a real point of hope! An example is Philippians 3:20,21 - *"But our citizenship is in heaven, and from it we await a Savior, the Lord Jesus Christ, who will transform our lowly body to be like his glorious body, by the power that enables him even to subject all things to himself."* The classic Pauline passage is 1 Corinthians 15:42-44, 49-57 - *"So is it with the resurrection of the dead. What is sown is perishable; what is raised is imperishable. It is sown in dishonor; it is raised in glory. It is sown in weakness; it is raised in power. It is sown a natural body; it is raised a spiritual body."....."Just as we have borne the image of the man of dust, we shall also bear the image of the man of heaven. I tell you this, brothers: flesh and blood cannot inherit the kingdom of God, nor does the perishable inherit the imperishable. Behold! I tell you a mystery. We shall not all sleep, but we shall all be changed, in a moment, in the twinkling of an eye, at the last trumpet. For the trumpet will sound, and the dead will be raised imperishable, and we shall be changed. For this perishable body must put on the imperishable, and this mortal body must put on immortality. When the perishable puts on the imperishable, and the mortal puts on immortality, then shall come to pass the saying that is written:*

"Death is swallowed up in victory." "O death, where is your victory? O death, where is your sting?"

The sting of death is sin, and the power of sin is the law. But thanks be to God, who gives us the victory through our Lord Jesus Christ." Sin, death, and our corruptible nature has been conquered in Christ! This is the hope we have when we've placed our faith in Christ alone for salvation. Do you have this 'hope of glory'? If not, repent and place your trust in Christ and present yourself to be discipled in the fellowship of his church.

COLOSSIANS 3:5-11

"Put to death therefore what is earthly in you: sexual immorality, impurity, passion, evil desire, and covetousness, which is idolatry. On account of these the wrath of God is coming. In these you too once walked, when you were living in them. But now you must put them all away: anger, wrath, malice, slander, and obscene talk from your mouth. Do not lie to one another, seeing that you have put off the old self with its practices and have put on the new self, which is being renewed in knowledge after the image of its creator. Here there is not Greek and Jew, circumcised and uncircumcised, barbarian, Scythian, slave, free; but Christ is all, and in all. Put on then, as God's chosen ones, holy and beloved, compassionate hearts, kindness, humility, meekness, and patience, bearing with one another and, if one has a complaint against another, forgiving each other; as the Lord has forgiven you, so you also must forgive. And above all these put on love, which binds everything together in perfect harmony. And let the peace of Christ rule in your hearts, to which indeed you were called in one body. And be thankful. Let the word of Christ dwell in you richly, teaching and admonishing one another in all wisdom, singing psalms and hymns and spiritual songs, with thankfulness in your hearts to God. And whatever you do, in word or deed, do everything in the name of the Lord Jesus, giving thanks to God the Father through him (Col. 3:5-17)."

7

Put to Death Therefore

We've now come to an extended section of ethical appeals. Paul has spent two chapters establishing the theological underpinnings for his appeals, so there's a clear shift of focus and a change in the nature of the discussion from considering what God has provided for us in Christ to thinking about how these provisions should reshape the way we live. This is typical of Paul's writing and a good example of applied theology. Theological understanding that is unrelated to real life and human behavior is a useless exercise and empty of any practical value. But the understandings Paul has put forward in the past chapters are both true and related to the demands of daily life. True conversion and understanding who we are in Christ will, in fact, transform our character and reorder the way we live. By way of reminder, verses 1-4 of chapter 3 underscore the reorientation of the Christian's mind and will, and then in verses 5-17 Paul calls for a new ethic, one that gives moral expression to the Christian's new mentality.

LANGUAGE & DISTINCTIONS

Before we go any further I want to preface our discussion by reminding you of some important language and theological distinctions made in Scripture. This is actually the language of the church which has been, to a large extent, abandoned in an effort to make the biblical message more accessible to those sitting in the pews. But, in actuality, what's happened is that essential theological ideas have become blurred and the full impact of the gospel has been weakened. There are three theological categories that need to be understood by every Christian: regeneration; justification; and sanctification. Regeneration is a sovereign act of divine quickening whereby we're brought to life, spiritually, and enabled to believe the gospel. It's God's work alone, and it precedes faith rather than being produced by faith. Regeneration is God's gift of spiritual birth. Justification is an act of divine declaration in which God pronounces as righteous those he's regenerated solely on the merits of Christ. This too is God's work alone! Sanctification is growth in Christ, and it's a cooperative project requiring those who have been regenerated and justified to apply themselves in sustained obedience. In sanctification we're certainly not self-reliant, but it's equally true that we're not passive participants in the process. Sanctification calls for 'God dependent effort (J.I. Packer)'. Paul states this clearly in Romans 6 - *"....For just as you once presented your members as slaves to impurity and to lawlessness leading to more lawlessness, so now present your members as slaves to righteousness leading to sanctification (v.19)."* We're expected to participate in our sanctification by making every effort to grow in Christ. What we discover is that sanctification comes by way of spiritual struggle and moral conflict. Even though our sinful appetites have been dethroned, they're not yet destroyed. We've been enabled, by regeneration to identify and resist the impulses of our sinfulness and grow in Christian holiness. This is where confusion often develops. There is a tendency to not make a clear distinction between justification and sanctification. We think that the moral and ethical demands that are appropriate to the process of sanctification are actually required for our justification. Not true! We must be careful and not allow the demands of sanctification to bleed into our understanding of justification.

We're now in a position to begin discussing the ethical section of Colossians, which falls into the category of Christian sanctification. The transition from theology to ethics pivots on the conjunction 'therefore' in verse 5 - *"Put to death therefore what is earthly in you..."* The 'therefore' signals a crucial 'reach back' to verses 1-4. A connection is being made between the line in verse 3 - *"For you have died..."* - with the line in verse 5 - *"Put to death therefore what is earthly in you;..."* Put to death what is sinful and foreign to your new nature. Stated more positively, the appeal is that we become what we are, a righteous people by divine decree. There are moral expectations that come with being in union with Christ and legally repositioned in his death and resurrection. You can see this clearly in verse 1 - *"If [since] then you have been raised with Christ, seek the things that are above,....."* It's expected that if we're truly converted we'll have a reorientation of mind and will. We'll have a desire to please God and a distaste for those things that displease him. Our union with Christ demands that we 'put to death' sinful vices. And there are particular ones identified that were probably prominent in Gentile circles. First, sexual sin - *"...sexual immorality, impurity, passion, evil desire and covetousness, which is idolatry (v.5)."* Then there are relational sins - *"...anger, wrath, malice, slander, and obscene (degrading) talk from your mouth (v.8)."* We find similar sinful clusters throughout the New Testament (Eph.5:5; 1 Cor.5:10, 6:9; Rev.21:8, 22:15).

THREE NOTATIONS

There are three notations made here that are important to see:

first, sexual sin is an expression of idolatry. It's a driving desire to have more and more sexual experiences and pleasures which crowd God out of the center of our lives. Second, sinful practices are subject to God's future wrath (v.6), and divine judgment is a dreadful thing to consider. Third, prior to coming to Christ, we were all held captive to sinful passions and immoral appetites. In fact, we once walked and lived in them. They defined us morally. The sensual dominated our desires and determined our behaviors. We were enslaved to sin.

Now that we're 'in Christ' we're no longer under obligation to the sinful practices of the 'old self.' Our union with Christ not only demands that we turn away from these sinful practices, but it also empowers us to do so. Paul on this point - *"For if you live according to the flesh you will die, but if by the Spirit you put to death the deeds of the body, you will live (Rom.8:13)."* The Apostle John speaks to the same point, but in a more provocative way - *"Everyone who makes a practice of sinning also practices lawlessness; sin is lawlessness. You know that he appeared in order to take away sins, and in him there is no sin. No one who abides in him keeps on sinning; no one who keeps on sinning has either seen him or known him. Little children, let no one deceive you. Whoever practices righteousness is righteous, as he is righteous. Whoever makes a practice of sinning is of the devil, for the devil has been sinning from the beginning. The reason the Son of God appeared was to destroy the works of the devil. No one born of God makes a practice of sinning, for God's seed abides in him; and he cannot keep on sinning, because he has been born of God. By this it is evident who are the children of God, and who are the children of the devil: whoever does not practice righteousness is not of God, nor is the one who does not love his brother (1 Jn.3:4-10)."* The point we need to take away from this is that if we've been 'born of God', intentional and habitual sinning will grieve us and we'll be striving to see long established patterns of sinfulness broken in our lives. We'll be engaged in the struggles of sanctification by striving to put off "the old self with its practices" and put on "the new self that is being renewed in knowledge after the image of its creator (v.10)."

TRANSFORMED

There is a dynamic and growing edge involved when conversion is real and we're truly identified with Christ's death and resurrection. When we're 'in him' we're enlivened by the Holy Spirit, awakened to the things of God, and we will be sanctified. Our character and moral life is being transformed over time. If you're a true Christian you will be changed; but the pace and degree of that change will vary from person to person. Christian sanctification is God's transforming work in us occurring over time, radically altering our habits of mind and life as we pursue and present ourselves to him.

In the last line of verse 10 there are several things regarding sanctification indicated - *"....which is being renewed in knowledge after the image of its creator."* The verb, 'being renewed', is a present participle telling us that sanctification is a process. We're becoming! Then we have two prepositional phrases, 'in knowledge' and 'after the image'. The renewal of the 'new self' is stimulated by an ever increasing knowledge of God in Christ. 'Knowledge' (ἐπίγνωσις) is relational knowing - participation in the object known - not a detached intellectual knowing. Also, the 'new self' is renewed *"...after the image of its creator."* This renewal is a re-conforming to God's original intention for us, that in our humanity the image of God would be clearly expressed (Gen.1:26,27). In redemption then we have a 'new creation' mediated through and patterned after Christ himself. Paul states this plainly in Romans 8:29 - *"For those whom he foreknew he also predestined to be conformed to the image of his Son,..."*

This paragraph closes with the expansion of this idea of the 'new self'; it has broader implications and impact than just on the individual believer alone. The gospel creates a new humanity, a new community, a new corporate 'self'; what Paul refers to in Ephesians as 'one new man', the 'mystery of Christ'. This new humanity is radically inclusive, it's blind to the ethnic, racial, and social distinctions that create divisions and strife among men. In this new community (the church) solidarity in Christ is what's most important - "Here [within the realm of the new man] there is *"...not Greek and Jew, circumcised and uncircumcised, barbarian (non-Greeks considered culturally inferior), Scythians, slave, free; but Christ is all, and all (v.11)."* This is a profound idea that within the culture of the church the polarizing tendencies characteristic of the fallen world are overcome. What creates this solidarity and peace is Christ! It's a renewed human condition created in Christ through the gospel, or as Paul states it - *"Christ is all".* He's absolutely everything; he's all that matters, because it's in him that all things, both in creation and redemption, are held together (Col.1:17). Also, in this new community Christ is 'in all'; he indwells all those who have placed their faith in him. He's the binding thread of commonality that causes this new humanity to be blind to skin color and class. This is the profound nature of Christian salvation; it changes us, it empowers us, and it creates a 'new self', transforming the believer's character and life.

COLOSSIANS 3:12-17

"Put on then, as God's chosen ones, holy and beloved, compassionate hearts, kindness, humility, meekness, and patience, bearing with one another and, if one has a complaint against another, forgiving each other; as the Lord has forgiven you, so you also must forgive. And above all these put on love, which binds everything together in perfect harmony. And let the peace of Christ rule in your hearts, to which indeed you were called in one body. And be thankful. Let the word of Christ dwell in you richly, teaching and admonishing one another in all wisdom, singing psalms and hymns and spiritual songs, with thankfulness in your hearts to God. And whatever you do, in word or deed, do everything in the name of the Lord Jesus, giving thanks to God the Father through him."

8

Put on Then

Colossians chapter 3 is a call to sanctification in which Paul appeals to us to develop a heavenly perspective on the whole of life since we've been 'raised with Christ' and are now spiritually alive and no longer enslaved to sin. This heavenly perspective is to be fleshed out in particular ways. Specific vices and sinful attitudes are to be 'put away' (vv.5,8), and we're given a list of virtues that are to be 'put on'. Also, we should keep in mind that in verses 10 and 11 Paul expands the idea of the 'new self' so that it's no longer limited to the individual; rather it's also a corporate reference referring to a new humanity, the 'one new man', the church. And this community is radically inclusive, it's blind to the common ethnic, racial, and social distinctions that create divisions and strife among men. It's a redeemed community whose solidarity and peace is the result of Christ being 'all and in all (v.11)'. He's the center and source of our fellowship, and he indwells all those who've placed their faith in him. It's Christ who makes us blind to color and class. As we consider this paragraph, we need to keep in mind that the discussion is still on the corporate nature of the 'new self'; so there are certain vices that we need to turn away from because they create dissension within the Christian community (vv.8,9). But there are virtues that need to be 'put on' because they nurture and sustain peace within the church (vv.12-14).

RE-IDENTIFIERS

The first thing we're confronted with in this passage are three re-identifiers. As Christians we're no longer defined by the 'old self' which is self-centered and self-possessed. We're now God's 'chosen ones', 'holy and beloved'. Our self-understanding is shaped, not by a radical individualism, but by a keen awareness that we're part of a new community. Not new in the sense of just beginning having never existed before, but new in a qualitative, broadened sense. This 'new self' - this new humanity - in actuality is an enlarged Israel. The identifiers used in verse 12 are also used to identify Old Testament Israel; they were God's chosen people who were holy and loved. The same is true of the New Covenant church, which Paul refers to as 'spiritual Israel'; but it's not associated with any particular nation or race. There is true racial and cultural diversity within the church. The New Testament church is made up of every race and people from every ethnic and cultural background, and yet they share these fundamental identifiers; they're God's 'chosen ones' and they're 'holy and beloved'.

The identifier 'God's chosen ones' tells us that God is the active party in salvation. He pursues us, not we him, and every one of his people is hand selected. His 'chosen ones' are holy, they're set apart to God, and they're dearly loved. Together these identifiers speak of divine election. This is a prominent theme throughout Scripture - *"Behold, to the Lord your God belong heaven and the heaven of heavens, the earth with all that is in it. Yet the Lord set his heart in love on your fathers and chose their offspring after them, you above all peoples, as you are this day"....."For you are a people holy to the Lord your God, and the Lord has chosen you to be a people for his treasured possession, out of all the peoples who are on the face of the earth (Deut.10:14, 15; 14:2)."* This is also expressed throughout all of Paul's writings, for example - *"But we ought always to give thanks to God for you, brothers beloved by the Lord, because God chose you as the firstfruits to be saved, through sanctification by the Spirit and belief in the truth. To this he called you through our gospel, so that you may obtain the glory of our Lord Jesus Christ (2 Thess.2:13,14)."* This doctrine of divine election is both disturbing and reassuring; it's disturbing because it makes it plain that we're not in charge, and it causes us to wonder why some are chosen and others are not. There is a deep mystery here! But it's also reassuring because when you understand the profound nature of the 'Fall', and acknowledge that apart from Christ we're utterly dead spiritually, then it becomes clear that if God doesn't break into our despairing condition and save some, we all would be lost. Inherent in his redemptive intervention is divine election. It's a mysterious expression of grace!

VIRTUES

As 'God's chosen ones' we're to pursue five virtues (v.12) which serve as counter-points to five vices (v.8). What these virtues do is nurture and sustain a healthy community. Each of these is a positive relationship building trait.

- 'Compassionate hearts' - a love characterized by mercy.
- 'Kindness' - goodness expressed through gracious acts.
- 'Humility' - valuing others above ourselves.
- 'Meekness' - not self-promoting.
- 'Patience' - restrained reaction to offenses.

Do these seem familiar? Each of these virtues is attributed to Christ. In a very real sense Paul is saying here what he said to the Romans - *"...put on the Lord Jesus Christ... (Rom.13:14)."* Grow in Christ, sincerely present yourself to God, and pursue your sanctification. As these virtues are formed in us they equip us to bear with one another and forgive each other. Given the inclusive nature of the church, both of these expressions - bearing with and forgiving - are crucial to maintaining harmony and peace within the Christian community. Notice that we're to forgive because we're forgiven (v.13). There is moral obligation involved in the command to forgive. Christ provides both the model and the reason to forgive - *"...forgiving each other; as [because] the Lord has forgiven you, so you also just forgive."* Christian forgiveness is motivated by something greater than personal feelings; it's an expression of Christ's character and our gratitude to God. Love is what enlivens each of the stated virtues causing them to contribute to the relational harmony of the church - *"...above all these (over all these) put on love, which binds everything together in perfect harmony (v.14)."*

LEGITIMATE APPEALS

Given that we're striving to grow in Christ and develop these Christ-like virtues, the closing appeals can be legitimately made - *"....let the peace of Christ rule in your hearts...(v.15)"* and *"Let the word of Christ dwell in you richly...(v.16)."* Both of these appeals have a bearing on the church and Christian relationships. The first exhorts us to let the relational peace that's both embodied in and provided by Christ be the controlling factor whenever there are competing interests in the life of the church. The question is: what will make for peace? Can compromises be made, or considerations extended that will resolve conflict over personal preferences while not compromising biblical truth or moral convictions? These situations often involve the delicate edges of relationships that demand that we yield and lay aside our own interests so that we don't offend, but we preserve peace. The Apostle Paul reminds us that we're members of one body, so when we disregard the sensibilities of others we're not walking in '*...love, which binds everything together in perfect harmony (v.14).*" He also gives similar instruction to the church in Rome - "*Therefore let us not pass judgment on one another any longer, but rather decide never to put a stumbling block or hindrance in the way of a brother. I know and am persuaded in the Lord Jesus that nothing is unclean in itself, but it is unclean for anyone who thinks it unclean. For if your brother is grieved by what you eat, you are no longer walking in love. By what you eat, do not destroy the one for whom Christ died. So do not let what you regard as good be spoken of as evil. For the kingdom of God is not a matter of eating and drinking but of righteousness and peace and joy in the Holy Spirit (Rom.14:13-17).*" Debatable things are matters of personal conscience or preference. Instead of pushing to get our own way we should just be thankful that we've been saved by the grace of God, and we're privileged to be part of the 'body of Christ.'

The second appeal compliments the first. Question: how do we promote the rule of the 'peace of Christ' in our relationships? Answer: by letting the 'word of Christ' dwell in us richly. The 'word of Christ' is the message that proclaims Christ; it's the gospel, the message of God's gracious provision in Christ. We're to let the gospel dwell in us richly; let it take up permanent residence in our lives by penetrating our character and transforming our approach to relationships. How is this rich indwelling of the gospel encouraged in our lives? By the thoughtful teaching of the gospel; by admonishing one another in the gospel; and by singing the gospel. The church that puts Christ and the gospel at the center of its worship and shared life will see the relationships of its people transformed because the more we love Christ, the more we'll love each other. As we gain understanding of the rich grace extended to us in Christ we become more gracious with each other. So rather than trying to gain petty advantage over each other our first impulse is to care for and encourage one another.

This paragraph closes with a line similar to the opening line of this extended section of exhortation. The section began in chapter 2 verse 6 with these words - *"Therefore, as you received Christ Jesus the Lord, so walk in him,..."* The section closes with these words - *"And whatever you do, in word or deed, do everything in the name of the Lord Jesus, giving thanks to God the Father through him (v.17)."* Put on the 'new self' and put off the old by growing in your understanding of the gospel, and strive to reflect the character of Christ through all of your attitudes and actions.

COLOSSIANS 3:18-4:1

"Wives, submit to your husbands, as is fitting in the Lord. Husbands, love your wives, and do not be harsh with them. Children, obey your parents in everything, for this pleases the Lord. Fathers, do not provoke your children, lest they become discouraged. Bondservants, obey in everything those who are your earthly masters, not by way of eye-service, as people-pleasers, but with sincerity of heart, fearing the Lord. Whatever you do, work heartily, as for the Lord and not for men, knowing that from the Lord you will receive the inheritance as your reward. You are serving the Lord Christ. For the wrongdoer will be paid back for the wrong he has done, and there is no partiality. Masters, treat your bondservants[b] justly and fairly, knowing that you also have a Master in heaven."

9

Household Rules & True Spirituality

This section of Paul's letter to the Colossians is a stand alone unit made up of a series of admonitions governing relationships in the Christian household. It's a series of household rules, which was common among both Jews and Gentiles. This household code addresses three pairs of people: wives and husbands, children and fathers (parents), and slaves and masters. There is a shared pattern to each admonition. The party that it's directed to is named, a command is given, and a statement of motivation is made.

Before examining each of these admonitions more closely, I want to frame our thinking about them in a particular way. There's a common comment made by people when asked about their religious persuasion; many will say that they're 'spiritual' but not religious. When they say they're not religious it's understood that they're not adhering to any institutionalized set of religious beliefs, and not associated with any organized religion. Being 'spiritual' is a much less precise reference, it can mean anything from being curious about the paranormal to practicing yoga and entertaining secularized Buddhist ideas. Yet, one thing is clear; being 'spiritual' is highly individualized and it's considered good; whereas being 'religious' is passe', conformist, restrictive, and not necessarily good. If you announce that you're a 'spiritual' person, you'll be received with applause, but if you say you're religious you'll be greeted with a yawn or a clenched fist. One thing is certain, developing your 'spirituality' is very much in vogue today.

Let's rewind history all the way back to first century Colossae and ask the question: 'What did trendy spirituality look like then?' Apparently it involved the mixing of Christian, pagan, and Jewish ideas. In practice, it involved asceticism, mystical experiences, visions, and spiritual mysteries. The beliefs of the false teachers in Colossae certainly challenged the sufficiency of Christ's saving work. Also, they remained varied and somewhat fluid and open to personalized interpretation, perhaps in an effort to mitigate the wrong-headed spirituality of the false teachers. Paul inserts this set of 'household rules' and says, 'if you want to understand the nature of Christian spirituality, look closely at the mundane, domestic relationships in the Christian household. True spirituality isn't 'other-worldly' in the sense of being disassociated from the demands and exactions of daily life. In reality, that's where it's put on display. Christian spirituality has everything to do with a present 'well-lived' life, one that transforms the ordinary and makes it extraordinary.

FOUNDATIONAL THINGS

Before we look more closely at these transformed household relationships, there are several foundational things that need to be noted. The first is that as Christians, our spirituality isn't the result of self-generated disciplines; rather, the proot of Christian spirituality is a thoughtful understanding of the gospel, or as Paul states it in chapter 2, verses 2&3, it flows out of *"....the riches of full assurance of understanding and the knowledge of God's mystery, which is Christ, in whom are hidden all the treasures of wisdom and knowledge."* The more we understand what has been provided for us in Christ, and the deeper our devotion to him becomes, the more our way of living is transformed. God, by his Spirit, works through his Word to change the way we think and live. This forms the dynamic of Christian sanctification and spiritual life.

The second thing to note is that Christian living is motivated by an ambition to honor Christ in the whole of life - *"And whatever you do, in word or deed, do everything in the name of the Lord Jesus, giving thanks to God the Father through him (vv.3:17)."* Third, our earthly lives reflect a heavenly perspective - *"If (since) then you have been raised with Christ, seek the things that are above, where Christ is...set your minds on things that are above, not on things that are on earth (vv.3:1,2)."* Our temporal lives are to be reshaped by heavenly values and a heavenly way of seeing. Finally, our spirituality is expressed through relational mutuality and reciprocity. In the new humanity that's been created in Christ there are no distinctions made based on race, ethnicity, or social class; rather, there's mutuality. In the Christian's earthly family the ruling principle that shapes the relationships of the household involves a fundamental reciprocity expressed through dutiful and complimenting exchanges between family members. Christian spirituality is clearly displayed in the reciprocity lived out among the members of the Christian household. So spirituality isn't an abstraction detached from real life activities; rather, it's woven into the fabric of everyday life. It's expressed in the concrete terms of human relationships, which is the most demanding category of human life.

THREE RELATIONSHIPS

We need to think about the three relationships presented in this passage, particularly as they embody and display Christian spirituality. We have three pairs of relationships mentioned: wives and husbands; children and parents; and slaves and masters. Given that slaves are included in the household it's clear that the first century household was quite different from today's nuclear family. Not only did it include parents and their young children, it often included older children and their spouses as well as domestic slaves. The primary relationship in the household was that of the husband and wife, and the spirituality produced by their living under the Lordship of Christ altered the nature of their relationship. In secular society wives were often treated as property by their husbands; they had no rights and were often mistreated. In this cultural context, Paul's instruction was radically countercultural. Not that he called for structural change in the social order, but that he called for change in the essential nature of those structures. The gospel isn't socially destructive, but it is socially transformative. Christian wives were to still acknowledge the headship of their husbands by submitting to their leadership. But they're not to submit simply because he was a harsh despot or because society demanded it; but rather, out of recognition of God's ordering of marriage, understanding that *"...the head of a wife is her husband...(1Cor.11:3)."* It's out of a desire to please the Lord and submit to his word that a Christian wife voluntarily places herself under the authority and direction of her husband. This subordination doesn't infer inferiority. Perhaps it's better understood in the sense of Philippians 2:3-4 - *"....in humility count others more significant than yourselves. Let each of you look not only to his own interests, but also to the interests of others."* This is what true spirituality looks like, it bears the face of submission and selfless service.

This same spiritual expression is required of Christian husbands as well - *"Husbands, love your wives and do not be harsh with them (v.19)."* This is extraordinary instruction that was completely absent from Greek and Jewish house codes. When a husband is truly converted and begins to display the 'mind of Christ' he recognizes that he's required to love his wife *"...as Christ loved the church and gave himself up for her,...(Eph.5:25)."* This call for self-sacrificing love mitigates the misuse of authority and marital headship. So, a husband will often defer to the interests and needs of his wife without abandoning or compromising his responsibilities of leadership. In a Christian marriage spirituality is expressed through relational reciprocity, through submission and sacrificial service rather than self-will and abusive domination. The same dynamic is called for in the parent-child relationship - *"Children, obey your parents in everything, for this pleases the Lord. Fathers (parents), do not provoke (embitter) your children, lest they become discouraged (vv.20,21)."* This instruction is easily understood. Children of all ages who are living in a parent's home are to honor their parents and respect the household rules. Again, there's reciprocity here, parents aren't to exasperate their children by making demands that cause their children to lose heart and give up trying to please them. Christian maturity and true spirituality are expressed through submission and selfless service out of obedience to Christ.

The final category of relationships spoken of by the Apostle is that of 'masters and slaves' - *"Bondservants, obey in everything those who are your earthly masters, not by way of eye-service, as people-pleasers, but with sincerity of heart, fearing the Lord. Whatever you do, work heartily, as for the Lord and not for men, knowing that from the Lord you will receive the inheritance as your reward. You are serving the Lord Christ. For the wrongdoer will be paid back for the wrong he has done, and there is no partiality. Masters, treat your bondservants justly and fairly, knowing that you also have a Master in heaven (vv.3:22-41)."* A side note: don't read into

Paul's comments any endorsement of institutional slavery; he's simply speaking to the social conditions as they were. The instruction that's given to slaves, or domestic servants, suggests that there was confusion in the minds of Christian servants as to how the mutuality they were experiencing in the church should affect their standing in the Christian household. Notice where their loyalty is ultimately directed; it's to the Lord - *"...obey...fearing the Lord (v.22)"...."...work heartily, as for the Lord...(v.23)"...."knowing that from the Lord you will receive the inheritance...(v.24)"..."You are serving the Lord Christ (v.24)."* They are being told by Paul to submit to their master's authority and serve them as an expression of their commitment to Christ. Ultimately, their obedience and selfless servanthood is directed to Christ under whose Lordship they live. It should also be noted that a master's authority isn't absolute; it's restrained by an awareness that he too is accountable to his 'Master in heaven' (v.4:1). He's to treat his servants justly and fairly. There's a reciprocal element underscored in the relationship that checks the potential abuses of the relationship.

CHRISTIAN SPIRITUALITY

What is displayed in this set of 'household rules' is the character of Christian spirituality. It's grounded in Christ and his Lordship, and expressed through concrete acts of submission and service. It's relational in nature and recognizes the established social structures of every time period and culture, but subverts them and transforms them over time. This is why abusive forms of marriage and parenting, as well as institutional slavery can't stand where the voice of the gospel is strong. False spirituality is superficial, prideful, and self-promoting; whereas true Christian spirituality is self-forgetful, Christ-centered, and life transforming.

COLOSSIANS 4:2-6

"Continue steadfastly in prayer, being watchful in it with thanksgiving. At the same time, pray also for us, that God may open to us a door for the word, to declare the mystery of Christ, on account of which I am in prison— that I may make it clear, which is how I ought to speak. Walk in wisdom toward outsiders, making the best use of the time. Let your speech always be gracious, seasoned with salt, so that you may know how you ought to answer each person."

10

Prayer & Christian Witness

These are final words of instruction to a church at risk and a group of Christians for whom Paul has great concern, even though he's never met them. So this final set of admonitions has significance and weight. We need to pay attention to the final things people say. They tend to be important and often expose matters of urgency and a person's priorities of heart. For Paul two points of urgency are exposed here, and simply stated in two lines of text - *"Continue steadfastly in prayer,...(v.2)"...."Walk in wisdom toward outsiders,...(v.5)."* Prayer is important to Paul, and is encouraged frequently in his correspondence with individuals and churches. For Paul, prayer is to be a prominent part of Christian life. Christians are to be praying people. And yet, Paul doesn't set prayer goals, in terms of hours spent or established times of prayer each day. He simply says *"Continue steadfastly in prayer,..."* Prayer is to be habitual. We're to be a prayerful people, praying regularly. Praying privately and corporately, praying formally and informally. It should be daily but the exact length of time and the placement of prayer in the schedule of our day varies with each individual and is a matter of personal conscience and the demands of our daily lives. However, I don't think any of us is in danger of over-praying. I know I'll never be called 'old camel knees' as the Apostle John was because of the damage done to his knees by the hours he spent in prayer.

WATCHFUL & THANKFUL

There are some features of prayer that should be part of all of our prayer lives. The first mentioned is that our prayer lives should feature 'watchfulness' and 'thanksgiving' - *"...being watchful in it (prayer) with thanksgiving...(v.2)."* What does Paul mean when he says 'being watchful' in prayers? The verb 'watchful' is also translated 'awake' or 'alert'. It's often used in the New Testament in the sense of staying spiritually alert since Christ could return at any time. A good example of this is found in 1 Thessalonians 5:1-6 - *"Now concerning the times and the seasons, brothers, you have no need to have anything written to you. For you yourselves are fully aware that the day of the Lord will come like a thief in the night. While people are saying, "There is peace and security," then sudden destruction will come upon them as labor pains come upon a pregnant woman, and they will not escape. But you are not in darkness, brothers, for that day to surprise you like a thief. For you are all children of light, children of the day. We are not of the night or of the darkness. So then let us not sleep, as others do, but let us keep awake (watchful) and be sober."* This isn't a call to a speculative preoccupation with the Second Coming, but rather, to a watchfulness over our own lives in light of the imminent return of Christ. Recognizing that this time period between the first and second comings of Christ is a period of great danger and spiritual conflict, we need to be constantly in prayer, spiritually alert, and guarding our souls. Peter speaks poignantly to this point - *"Humble yourselves, therefore, under the mighty hand of God so that at the proper time he may exalt you, casting all your anxieties on him, because he cares for you. Be sober-minded; be watchful. Your adversary the devil prowls around like a roaring lion, seeking someone to devour. Resist him, firm in your faith, knowing that the same kinds of suffering are being experienced by your brotherhood throughout the world. And after you have suffered a little while, the God of all grace, who has called you to his eternal glory in Christ, will himself restore, confirm, strengthen, and establish you. To him be the dominion forever and ever. Amen (1Pet.5:6-11)."*

Not only are we to be 'watchful', we're also to be 'thankful'. This disposition is called for often in Colossians. In the opening section of the letter Paul writes - *"...giving thanks to the Father, who has qualified you to share in the inheritance of the saints in light (v.1:12)."* This appeal is also made in chapters 2 and 3 - *"Therefore, as you received Christ Jesus the Lord, so walk in him, rooted and built up in him and established in the faith, just as you were taught, abounding in thanksgiving"..."And let the peace of Christ rule in your hearts, to which indeed you were called in one body. And be thankful. Let the word of Christ dwell in you richly, teaching and admonishing one another in all wisdom, singing psalms and hymns and spiritual songs, with thankfulness in your hearts to God. And whatever you do, in word or deed, do everything in the name of the Lord Jesus, giving thanks to God the Father through him (vv.2:6,7; 3:15-17)."* Why should we be a thankful people? Here are just a few reasons why: we were once dead in our sins, but now we're forgiven and made spiritually alive in Christ. We once had no hope in the face of death, but we've now been gifted eternal life and can face the future with confidence and eager expectation. In the past, we were living under the impending judgment of God, but now we're covered and protected by God's grace. Are you thankful? You certainly have reason to be!

PRAYER AS PETITION

Notice that the nature of prayer is petitionary - *"....pray also for us (v.3)."* Paul's asking the Colossians to pray for him and Timothy, and all those associated with them in the gospel. He's asking them to pray especially for his ministry, and specifically that God would give him opportunities to preach the gospel - *"...that God may open to us a door for the word, to declare the mystery of Christ...(v.3)."* This is a clear reminder to us that we should be praying for opportunities to bear witness to Christ, and when doors open to us pray that we'll speak clearly and tactfully. And yet, look more closely at the language of the text. Paul's requesting prayer not just for opportunities to proclaim the gospel, but also that God, by his grace, will prepare the hearts of hearers to receive it in faith - *"...that God may open to us a door for the word,..."* [for the reception of the word]. Listen, the saving dynamic of the gospel isn't in its messenger, it's in its message. The gospel is *"...the power of God for salvation...(Rom.1:16)."* The Holy Spirit uses the message of the gospel to save, not the eloquence or persuasiveness of the messenger. Also, one thing is made very clear, Paul is passionate about the gospel and he's devoted to Christ, who is the embodiment of the gospel. This becomes obvious in the last line of verse 3 - *"... on account of which I am in prison."* Paul is under house arrest in Rome for preaching the gospel, or as he refers to it; for declaring *"the mystery of Christ."* It's interesting that Paul speaks of the gospel as 'the mystery of Christ.' It indicates that redemptive truth, hidden in the past, has now been fully revealed in Christ. In the book of Ephesians, Paul uses the same phrase in reference to the radical idea that 'in Christ' Gentiles are included in the New Covenant fulfillment of the Old Testament redemptive promise. Jews and Gentiles alike are saved by placing their faith in Christ alone for salvation, and they become 'one new man', or a new kind of humanity. Earlier in Colossians Paul refers to this mystery as *"...Christ in you, the hope of glory (v.1:27)."* Christ indwells his people by the Holy Spirit and gives us confidence in our future glory, the fact that we'll be people of greater substance in the future. We'll be more substantially human than we are now, as mere shadows of what we were created to be.

In chapter 2, Paul again refers to the mystery and says this about it - *"which is Christ (v.2:2)."* The redemptive revelation is found simply in the person and work of Christ; he embodies a complete salvation. Everything necessary for man's salvation, and the restoration of the Cosmos is found in Jesus. These are just three examples of the variegated nature of the gospel, and we're to pray that God will open doors of opportunity for us to proclaim it, and that he'll prepare hearts to receive it in true repentance and faith.

Final thought: Paul is asking the Colossians to pray that he'd make the gospel clear to those he witnessed to; he didn't want anything in his life or speech to hinder his gospel proclamation. And yet, he's in prison and his movement and opportunities are limited. But there's an underlying conviction that Paul has, and that is that nothing, including enemies or circumstances, can hinder the influence of the gospel when it's plainly preached. You can hear this conviction coming through in his letter to Timothy, written during his final imprisonment in Rome - *"Remember Jesus Christ, risen from the dead, the offspring of David, as preached in my gospel, for which I am suffering, bound with chains as a criminal. But the word of God is not bound (2 Tim.2:8,9)!"* For this reason, Paul never gives up on the gospel, and he feels compelled to preach - *"...if I preach the gospel, that gives me no ground for boasting. For necessity is laid upon me. Woe to me if I do not preach the gospel (1Cor.9:16)."* How about you, do you feel compelled to bear witness to Christ?

A CALL TO EVANGELISM

The final two verses of the passage address this call to evangelism - *"Walk in wisdom toward outsiders, making the best use of the time. Let your speech always be gracious, seasoned with salt, so that you may know how you ought to answer each person (vv.5,6)."* Notice that there's no scripted presentation of the gospel here. The emphasis is placed on establishing good relationships with non-Christians ('outsiders') through the integrity of our lives and the tactfulness of our speech - *"Walk (live) in wisdom toward outsiders"..."Let your speech always be gracious,..."* We're to live upright lives and speak to unbelievers in winsome and gracious ways, ways that open conversations that will invite their questions and give us opportunities to share the story and good news of Christ with them. Dr. James Dunn, in his commentary on Colossians, writes that Paul envisioned a church - "expected to hold its own in the social setting of market place, baths, and meal table and to win attention by the attractiveness of its life and speech."[1] The most effective and natural way to do evangelism is to bear witness to others in the normal course and encounters of life, sharing the gospel with neighbors, family members, and co-workers. Perhaps the easiest way to evangelize is to invite someone to attend church with you, and then take them to lunch afterwards so you can have a conversation and answer their questions.

---

1   Dunn, James, *The Epistles to the Colossians and to Philemon,* (Wm. B. Eerdmans Publishing Co., Grand Rapids, MI.), p. 267.

We're called to pray, and give witness to Christ. Let's commit ourselves to prayer and to looking to the 'outside' for opportunities to share Christ with others. People need to hear the gospel!

"Tychicus will tell you all about my activities. He is a beloved brother and faithful minister and fellow servant in the Lord. I have sent him to you for this very purpose, that you may know how we are and that he may encourage your hearts, and with him Onesimus, our faithful and beloved brother, who is one of you. They will tell you of everything that has taken place here. Aristarchus, my fellow prisoner, greets you, and Mark, the cousin of Barnabas (concerning whom you have received instructions—if he comes to you, welcome him), and Jesus who is called Justus. These are the only men of the circumcision among my fellow workers for the kingdom of God, and they have been a comfort to me. Epaphras, who is one of you, a servant of Christ Jesus, greets you, always struggling on your behalf in his prayers, that you may stand mature and fully assured in all the will of God. For I bear him witness that he has worked hard for you and for those in Laodicea and in Hierapolis. Luke the beloved physician greets you, as does Demas. Give my greetings to the brothers at Laodicea, and to Nympha and the church in her house. And when this letter has been read among you, have it also read in the church of the Laodiceans; and see that you also read the letter from Laodicea. And say to Archippus, "See that you fulfill the ministry that you have received in the Lord." I, Paul, write this greeting with my own hand. Remember my chains. Grace be with you."

11

Final Greetings

This is a fairly standard conclusion to a letter written by Paul. It's straightforward and easily understood. And yet, when the passage is placed in the context of the whole letter it exposes some important understandings regarding the nature of the church. The church is the place where a remarkable interfacing of the divine and the human takes place. It's the place where human frailty and need is met with divine perfection and God's redemptive provision in Christ. By simply reading through the first two chapters of the book we become aware that we're dealing with divine revelation. What's presented aren't the ideas and understandings of a mere man. Let's go back and reread a few passages from the opening section of the book just to reconnect with the profound nature of what the Apostle Paul writes - *"being strengthened with all power, according to his glorious might, for all endurance and patience with joy; giving thanks to the Father, who has qualified you to share in the inheritance of the saints in light. He has delivered us from the domain of darkness and transferred us to the kingdom of his beloved Son, in whom we have redemption, the forgiveness of sins. He is the image of the invisible God, the firstborn of all creation. For by him all things were created, in heaven and on earth, visible and invisible, whether thrones or dominions or rulers or authorities—all things were created through him and for him. And he is before all things, and in him all things hold together. And he is the head of the body, the church. He is the beginning, the firstborn from the dead, that in everything he might be preeminent. For in him all the fullness of God was pleased to dwell, and through him to reconcile to himself all things, whether on earth or in heaven, making peace by the blood of his cross. And you, who once were alienated and hostile in mind, doing evil deeds, he has now reconciled in his body of flesh by his death, in order to present you holy and blameless and above reproach before him,"...."Now I rejoice in my sufferings for your sake, and in my flesh I am filling up what is lacking in Christ's afflictions for the sake of his body, that is, the church, of which I became a minister according to the stewardship from God that was given to me for you, to make the word of God fully known, the mystery hidden for ages and generations but now revealed to his saints. To them God chose to make known how great among the Gentiles are the riches of the glory of this mystery, which is Christ in you, the hope of glory"...."In him also you were circumcised with a circumcision made without hands, by putting off the body of the flesh, by the circumcision of Christ, having been buried with him in baptism, in which you were also raised with him through faith in the powerful working of God, who raised him from the dead. And you, who were dead in your trespasses and the uncircumcision of your flesh, God made alive together with him, having forgiven us all our trespasses, by canceling the record of debt that stood against us with its legal demands. This he set aside, nailing it to the cross. He disarmed the rulers and authorities and put them to open shame, by triumphing over them in him (vv. 1:11-22, 24-27; 2:11-15)."* These passages aren't the ordinary writings of a man. The insights presented here can't be the product of human imagination or a spiritual man's religious longings. There is nothing quite like them in the literary classics, or in the philosophical musings of men. These passages expose the extraordinary redemptive activities of God. This is divine revelation! And yet, these heavenly truths aren't unrelated to the common needs and struggles of man. As theologically lofty as chapters 1 and 2 are chapters 3 and 4 display the humanity of the church, a humanity fleshed out in moral character that's flawed, household relationships that are often strained, and the demands of religious life that are unkempt.

ENTRUSTED TO FRAIL HUMAN BEINGS

As I thought about this it reminded me of what Paul wrote to the Corinthian church. In his second letter sent to Corinth, he refers to the gospel as *"...the glory of Christ, who is the image of God (2 Cor.4:4)"*; then he goes on to say - *"...we have this treasure (the glorious gospel ministry and the empowering of the Holy Spirit) in jars of clay (2 Cor.4:7)."* The good news of Christ and the privilege of Apostolic ministry was entrusted to frail human beings. Why? - *"...to show that the surpassing power belongs to God and not to us."* So the relatedness of this divine revelation to the humanity of the church is purposeful. It's intended to underscore the greatness and graciousness of God and the God-centeredness of the gospel, so that we'll look outside of ourselves for salvation and give God the glory for it once it's received. What an unexpected association! On the one hand, the 'mystery of Christ' in all its wonder and nuanced beauty is entrusted to the church; on the other hand, the church is made up of flawed and fickle men and women commissioned to protect and proclaim the glorious gospel. We all come to the task in weakness, exercising varied and limited abilities, but none of us are self-contained and sufficient in ourselves. These are common Pauline themes. Two examples - *"For consider your calling, brothers: not many of you were wise according to worldly standards, not many were powerful, not many were of noble birth. But God chose what is foolish in the world to shame the wise; God chose what is weak in the world to shame the strong; God chose what is low and despised in the world, even things that are not, to bring to nothing things that are, so that no human being might boast in the presence of God. And because of him you are in Christ Jesus, who became to us wisdom from God, righteousness and sanctification and redemption, so that, as it is written, "Let the one who boasts, boast in the Lord"...."Such is the confidence that we have through Christ toward God. Not that we are sufficient in ourselves to claim anything as coming from us, but our sufficiency is from God, who has made us sufficient to be ministers of a new covenant, not of the letter but of the Spirit. For the letter kills, but the Spirit gives life (1 Cor.1:26-31; 2 Cor. 3:4-6)."* Embodied in the very nature of the church, which is composed of weak, despised, and incapable people, is a living metaphor of the nature of Christian salvation; a salvation that's gifted to the weak, the despised, and the incapable. Salvation is not given on the basis of our moral merit or our human achievements; salvation is solely the gift of God's grace.

JEWS & GENTILES NAMED

The listing of Paul's co-workers that we find in this closing passage illustrates the points made in the Corinthian passages I've cited above. When you look closely at the list of co-workers Paul provides, you can see the rich diversity and radical inclusiveness of the gospel and the church. In verses 10-14 there are three Jews and three Gentiles named. The Jewish converts are Aristarchus, Mark, and Justus. The Gentile converts are Epaphras, Luke, and Demas. The gospel calls both Jews and Gentiles to repentance and faith in Christ. Even though the backstories associated with each of these individuals are, no doubt, quite different, they all needed the saving grace God provides in Christ alone. Not only is there racial and ethnic inclusion in the church, there is also social inclusion. Rich and poor, slave and free, find equal standing before God in Christ and equal acceptance in the life of his church. For this reason, we have Onesimus and Luke mentioned without any distinction made between them, even though Onesimus was a runaway slave and Luke was an educated physician. This is what the church should look like! And yet, this openness to racial, ethnic, and social inclusion isn't perfectly expressed because of the humanity of the church. This is exposed in rather glaring terms in the notation we find in verse 11 - *"...These are the only men of the circumcision among my fellow workers for the kingdom of God,..."* Paul had been specifically called to preach the gospel to the Gentiles which was a very controversial claim in a church that was predominantly Jewish and had a strong negative attitude toward Gentiles. Even though Paul's outreach to Gentiles had been endorsed by church leadership it was still viewed with suspicion and was resisted by many in the Jewish population of the church. Of the thousands of Jews who had become Christians, only three joined with Paul in his efforts to evangelize the Gentiles: Aristarchus, Mark, and Justus. The divine and the human are both influential in shaping the character and witness of the church. So the perfections of Christ and his redemptive work are dulled by the humanity of man. It's only after the return of Christ that we'll be fully freed from the implications of the 'fall' and express the perfections of Christ perfectly. Don't expect a perfect church now, but certainly expect movement in the church toward that perfection that will be ours in the Age to come.

We also see in the co-workers of Paul differences in strength of character and depth of devotion to Christ. There are three men mentioned that illustrate this. The first is Demas who became notorious because of a single statement made by Paul in his second letter to Timothy - *"... Demas, in love with this present world, has deserted me... (2 Tim.4:10)."* This indictment came three to four years after the commendation Demas received here in Colossians. He had been a source of encouragement and comfort to Paul during his first imprisonment in Rome, but during his second Roman imprisonment Demas 'deserts' him. This is a strong word suggesting that Demas abandoned his commitments and obligations for no good reason other than that he loved this present world. This is a rather open statement with no specifics given, but it suggests that Demas had been enticed away from his commitment to gospel work by something of lesser value; a love for the 'present world': present pleasures, present opportunities, present achievements, present affluence, and present ease. Whatever it was, it exposed a weakness of character and a shallowness in Demas' devotion to Paul and their shared work, and more importantly his devotion to Christ. We don't know if he turned away from Christ completely, but we do know that he abandoned the work God had called him to. He was less passionate about Kingdom concerns than he once was. He'd been drawn away from endeavors that carried profound eternal consequences. How about you? Are you being enticed by the present world? The answer's 'yes', we all are, and everyday we have to decide how much we'll give way to the pressures of the present.

There are two men on the list who are the exact opposite of Demas in character and devotion: Epaphras and Aristarchus. Aristarchus is identified with a three word phrase - *"....my fellow prisoner...(v.10)."* We don't know how he became a prisoner in Rome with Paul, but it's very likely that he volunteered to join Paul in his house arrest in order to help him in his ongoing ministry. This is godly devotion! This is strength of character! Then there's Epaphras, the Colossian pastor. He's a man deeply devoted to his pastoral work - *"Epaphras, who is one of you, a servant of Christ Jesus, greets you, always struggling on your behalf in his prayers, that you may stand mature and fully assured in all the will of God. For I bear him witness that he has worked hard for you and for those in Laodicea and in Hierapolis (vv.4:12,13)."* Paul describes Epaphras as a 'servant of Christ Jesus' struggling in prayer and working hard on behalf of those under his pastoral care. Note: the verb 'worked' is not the common word for 'work' (ergon), but a rare word 'ponos' which is often translated 'pain'. Here it means 'work that involves much exertion and trouble'. Epaphras was devoted to Christ and deeply concerned about the spiritual welfare of those he pastored. So he labored and spent himself on their behalf.

Because of the humanness of the people God calls to Christ and allows to participate in the life of his church, there are going to be varied strengths of character and depth of devotion to Christ displayed. But those who acknowledge their weakness and cling to Christ will be made strong in him - *"...I will boast all the more gladly of my weakness....For when I am weak, then I am strong (2 Cor.12:9,10)."* Question: are you aware of your weaknesses and clinging to Christ?

VICTIMS OF SPIRITUAL AMBIVALENCE

This list contains the names of two other men of note: Archippus and Mark. Both of these men had fallen victim to spiritual ambivalence. They had both experienced God's call to ministry, and yet because of their humanness they were conflicted. Paul says regarding Archippus - *"...say to*

Archippus, 'See that you fulfill the ministry that you have received in the Lord' (v.17)." Apparently Archippus was tentative and hesitant to engage the ministry he'd been set apart for; perhaps out of self-doubt or fear. But he needed to embrace it, he needed to push past the obstacles and obey. This is a strong exhortation, but it's given in a spirit of encouragement. This is what inspires people to go forward in Christ and fulfill their call, not harsh criticism or hurtful indictments. Rather, we need to be challenged and affirmed. A good example of this is Mark who had abandoned Paul and Barnabas some twenty years prior, during their first missionary venture into Galatia. This led to a breach in the relationship of Paul and Barnabas resulting in Paul taking Silas with him on his second missionary trip and Barnabas taking Mark with him to Cyprus. It appears that this was providential because Mark grew and thrived under the care and encouragement of Barnabas, so that he's eventually reconciled to Paul. Now in Rome he's a great source of comfort and encouragement to Paul. The encouraged became the encourager. By God's grace mediated through the encouragement of others and by the empowering presence of his Holy Spirit, God transforms our ambivalence into decisiveness. God works through our human weaknesses to make us strong in him and to deepen our devotion and dependence on him, so that he'll receive all the glory. It's in this mysterious interface of divine grace and human weakness that God accomplishes his own purposes and will. We may never understand it fully, but we should learn to appreciate and celebrate it.

This is the nature of church and Christian life. We're living in the light of a perfect revelation. We're inspired by it and strengthened by it; and yet, we're frustrated by our humanity and the lingering consequences of sin. We find ourselves caught in the conflicts of flesh and spirit, sometimes to the point of despair. But we need to remember that these aren't signs of defeat, these are indicators of Christian growth. So keep on struggling, keep on growing, keep pressing forward, and adopt the determination of Paul who wrote - *"Not that I have already obtained this (conformity to Christ) or am already perfect, but I press on to make it my own, because Christ Jesus has made me his own (Phil.3:12)."* You're his! Be encouraged, and grow!

PHILEMON

12

Philemon

The book of Philemon is a personal note sent along with the letter to the Colossians to Philemon who was a prominent member of the church in Colossae. It appears that the Apostle Paul was well acquainted with Philemon, and because of the conversion of a runaway slave by the name of Onesimus Paul finds himself in the role of mediator and advocate on behalf of Onesimus because he was Philemon's slave. Apparently Onesimus had stolen from Philemon and fled for Rome hoping to get lost in city crowds and start a new life. But while on the run he's providentially brought under the witness of Paul. He's converted and discipled by the Apostle. Now he's being sent back to Colossae to face Philemon. Because he's in prison Paul can't accompany Onesimus, so he sends this note of appeal.

What lies behind the events that lead to the writing of this Apostolic note is perhaps the most important point to be made. Onesimus, after stealing from his master Philemon and fleeing to Rome, never intended to see Philemon again. He had taken his future into his own hands and set a self-determined course; and yet, he now finds himself on his way back to Philemon, converted and determined to face the man he had offended. What changed his course? God's providential intervention. As much as we'd like, we're not free in the sense of being completely autonomous. We're all dependent on God for our existence. And when it comes to his saving work in the world, it's always under his control from beginning to end. The Lord doesn't allow us to stumble along and accidentally encounter him. He's actively involved in the events leading to our conversion.

GOD'S SOVEREIGNTY

Onesimus' story is a wonderful example of God's sovereignty at work in redemption. Onesimus intended to be lost in the city crowds, but instead he's found, not by a tracker of runaway slaves, but by the Lord of glory. The Lord tracked him down, broke into his life, and brought him to repentance and faith in Christ. God constrained him and gave him the desire to surrender to Christ. God is always the pursuer in salvation. Jesus stated this plainly when he said - "You did not choose me, but I chose you...(Jn.15:16)." The same truth is inferred in Philemon 15 - "...this perhaps is why he was parted from you for a while,...". The Greek verb translated 'he was parted' is in the passive voice indicating that Onesimus' leaving Philemon involved more than his decision alone, he was being acted upon. He was separated from Philemon and laid hold of by Christ. God's at work in wonderful and mysterious ways. We can certainly resist God's redemptive dealings and push back. But if we've been 'parted' by him, he'll ultimately win!

Francis Thompson was addicted to opium and lived on the streets of London for three years. Through the love and care of Christians he was converted and wrote the autobiographical poem, *The Hound of Heaven.* The opening and closing lines of the poem are quite moving.

"I fled Him, down the nights and down the days; I fled him, down the arches of the years;

*I fled Him, down the labyrinthine ways of my own mind;
and in the midst of tears I hid from Him, and under running
laughter; Up vistaed hopes I sped; and shot, Precipitated,
down titanic glooms of chasmed fears, from those strong Feet
That followed, followed after.*

*But with unhurried chase, and unperturbed pace,
deliberate speed, majestic Instancy, they beat - and a Voice
beat more instant than the Feet - "All things betray thee,
who betrayest Me."......Rise, clasp My hand, and come! Halts
by me that footfall: Is my gloom, after all, Shade of His hand,
outstretched caressingly? Ah, fondest, blindest, weakest, I am
He Whom thou seekest!"*

The Psalmist David writes something similar -

*"Where shall I go from your Spirit?
Or where shall I flee from your presence?
If I ascend to heaven, you are there!
If I make my bed in Sheol, you are there!
If I take the wings of the morning
and dwell in the uttermost parts of the sea,
even there your hand shall lead me,
and your right hand shall hold me.
If I say, "Surely the darkness shall cover me,
and the light about me be night,"
even the darkness is not dark to you;
the night is bright as the day,
for darkness is as light with you (Ps.139:7-12)."*

APPLICATIONS

There are two other applications found in this story of
Onesimus and Philemon that I want to mention. One has

---

1   Francis Thompson, *The Hound of Heaven*, (houndofheaven.com/
poem).

to do with godly leadership, and the other speaks to the power of reconciliation. In the opening salutation there is an understated, yet crucial tact taken by Paul in order to successfully advocate for Onesimus. The issue at hand is a sensitive one, and Paul understood this. So his approach to Philemon is respectful and tactful. The opening greeting sets the tone and discloses the approach Paul's going to take - "Paul, a prisoner for Christ Jesus,....To Philemon our beloved fellow worker...(v.1)." This is a very different salutation than the one found in Colossians - "Paul, an apostle of Christ Jesus...(Col.1:1)." It appears that Paul didn't want to pull rank on Philemon by exercising his Apostolic authority; rather, he appeals to him as a 'fellow worker.' There's respect expressed here, and an understanding of Philemon's character. Paul consciously refuses to force a desired response from Philemon by bringing Apostolic pressure on him - *"Accordingly, though I am bold enough in Christ to command you to do what is required, yet for love's sake I prefer to appeal to you—I, Paul, an old man and now a prisoner also for Christ Jesus— I appeal to you for my child, Onesimus, whose father I became in my imprisonment...but I preferred to do nothing without your consent in order that your goodness might not be by compulsion but of your own accord (vv.8-10, 14)."* What a beautiful example of mature Christian leadership: not overbearing, not manipulative, not self-serving, only a desire to encourage and draw the best out of Philemon.

Also, Paul appeals to Philemon from a position of empathy and understanding. He presents himself as a 'prisoner for Christ Jesus.' He can say, 'Philemon, I know what it means to be violated and then forgive.' 'I know what it means to sacrifice and be misunderstood and engage in hard, costly discipleship.' 'So, I'm not asking you to do what I'm unwilling to do myself.' This is leadership with its sleeves rolled up! What Paul's engaged in is a crucial aspect of Christian leadership; he's setting an example. He not only gives instruction, he models what he's asking to be done. Living out our Christian convictions is what gives our witness integrity, whether that be in our homes, the work place, church, or in the larger community. The Christian leader is to lead from a position of respect, empathy, and example. Peter applies this specifically to pastors - *"So I exhort the elders among you, as a fellow elder and a witness of the sufferings of Christ, as well as a partaker in the glory that is going to be revealed: shepherd the flock of God that is among you, exercising oversight, not under compulsion, but willingly, as God would have you; not for shameful gain, but eagerly; not domineering over those in your charge, but being examples to the flock (1 Pet.5:1-3)."*

The final application I want to make from this passage has to do with the power of reconciliation. Martin Luther said that 'we're all God's Onesimi', we're all on the run and need to be reconciled to God as Onesimus was. But he probably never expected that he'd have to return to Colossae and be reconciled to Philemon. And yet, this is exactly what's required of him. He was to go and face Philemon, ask forgiveness, and make restitution. You can see these elements of reconciliation presented in several statements in the text - *"I am sending him back to you, sending my very heart...If he has wronged you at all, or owes you anything, charge that to my account. I, Paul, write this with my own hand: I will repay it—to say nothing of your owing me even your own self (vv.12, 18-19)."* It's important to understand that when we receive God's forgiveness we're not excused from having to face the consequences of our sin. We're obligated to make every effort to heal broken relationships and make restitution when appropriate. But, the demand for reconciliation wasn't only directed to Onesimus;

Philemon was also being asked to forgive. Socially, this was something a slave owner wasn't required or expected to do. To forgive and receive a runaway slave back sent the wrong message and threatened to destabilize the established social order of the day. Onesimus was a slave, Philemon was a slave owner. Their roles in society were well-defined and there were social expectations brought to bear on Philemon that challenged his character and call as a Christian. He was expected to severely punish Onesimus, but Paul appeals to him - *"Perhaps the reason he was separated from you for a little while was that you might have him back forever— no longer as a slave, but better than a slave, as a dear brother. He is very dear to me but even dearer to you, both as a fellow man and as a brother in the Lord. So if you consider me a partner, welcome him as you would welcome me (vv.15-17)."*

A BELOVED BROTHER

Paul is asking Philemon to resist social pressure by seeing Onesimus with new eyes, by acknowledging his personhood and human dignity, and by receiving him back, not as a slave but as a beloved Chriatian brother. This was radical stuff! Within the church, distinctions that accommodate pride and encourage prejudice are to be transformed by Christ into points of grace, mutual respect, and equality. The church is to provide the world with a prophetic witness to the character of the 'Age to come' where people from every race and culture and walk of life live together in peace under the Lordship of Christ. Real social and cultural change begins with genuine conversion which radically alters our way of seeing ourselves and the world. Also, it reshapes our attitude toward one another.

Packed into this little note from Paul to Philemon are a number of profound Christian understandings that should define us as God's people: redemptive providence, humble leadership, and radical reconciliation.

Final Thoughts

Colossians and Philemon have fed us true spiritual food. The theological instruction Paul gave us in Colossians formed the doctrinal grounding for the moral appeals he made in the closing section of the book. Understanding who Christ is and what he's done for us redemptively inspires us to live obedient lives and strive to be faithful followers of Christ. Paul is a good example; even while in prison he faithfully engaged in Apostolic ministry. His concern for a church he had never visited exposes his heart for the people of God and his '...anxiety for all the churches (2 Cor.11:28)." Paul faithfully proclaimed the gospel, revealing the 'mystery of Christ', in the harsh circumstances of imprisonment. His teaching and 'life-witness' is a source of inspiration and encouragement to us as 21st century believers.

The small Apostolic note to Philemon gives us insight into Paul's personal relationships. Addressing a sensitive situation with his friend Philemon, Paul is respectful and tactful. In a cultural environment that allowed slave owners to treat their slaves as 'human tools', Paul appeals to Philemon to be reconciled to his slave, Onesimus, as a 'beloved brother'. This was a radical request and witness to the life-transforming nature of Christian conversion. Conversion is a personal experience that carries profound social implications.

When read thoughtfully and prayerfully, Colossians and Philemon enrich our theological understanding and challenge us to live lives that are radicalized by the gospel. They deepen our understanding of what it means to think and live Christianly in the hostile environment of a 'fallen' world.

To Read Further

COLOSSIANS

Abbott, T. K. *A Critical and Exegetical Commentary on the Epistles to Ephesians and to the Colossians.* ICC. Edinburgh: T&T Clark, 1897.

Barth, Markus, and Helmut Blanke. Colossians: *A New Translation with Introduction and Commentary.* AB34B. New York: Doubleday, 1994.

Bruce, F. F. *The Epistles to the Colossians, to Philemon, and the Ephesians.* NICNT. Grand Rapids: Eerdmans, 1984.

Calvin, John. *The Epistles of Paul the Apostle to the Galatians, Ephesians, Philippians and Colossians.* Grand Rapids: Eerdmans, 1965.

Dunn, James D. G. *The Epistles to the Colossians and to Philemon.* NIGTC. Grand Rapids: Eerdmans, 1996.

Lightfoot, J. B. *Saint Paul's Epistles to the Colossians and to Philemon.* London: Macmillan, 1897. Reprint, Grand Rapids: Zondervan, 1971.

Martin, Ralph P. *Colossians and Philemon.* NCBC. Grand Rapids: Eerdmans, 1973.

Moo, Douglas J. *The Letters to the Colossians and to Philemon.* Grand Rapids: Eerdmans, 2008.

Moule, C. F. D. *The Epistles of Paul the Apostle to the Colossians and to Philemon.* CGTC. Cambridge: Cambridge University Press, 1968.

Wright, N. T. *The Epistles of Paul to the Colossians and to Philemon.* TNTC. Leicester, U.K.: Inter-Varsity, 1986.

PHILEMON

Barth, Markus, and Helmut Blanke. *The Letter to Philemon: A New Translation with Notes and Commentary.* Eerdmans Critical Commentary. Grand Rapids: Eerdmans, 2000.

Bruce, F. F. *The Epistles to the Colossians, to Philemon, and to the Ephesians.* NICNT. Grand Rapids: Eerdmans, 1996.

Dunn, James D. G. *The Epistles to the Colossians and to Philemon.* NIGTC. Grand Rapids: Eerdmans,1996.

Lightfoot, J. B. *Saint Paul's Epistles to the Colossians and to Philemon.* London: Macmillan, 1897 (repr., Grand Rapids: Zondervan, 1971).

Martin, Ralph P. *Colossians and Philemon.* NCBC. Grand Rapids: Eerdmans, 1973.

Moo, Douglas J. *The Letters to the Colossians and to Philemon.* Grand Rapids: Eerdmans, 2008.

Moule, C. F. D. *The Epistles of Paul the Apostle to the Colossians and to Philemon.* CGTC. Cambridge: Cambridge University Press, 1968.

Wright, N. T. *The Epistles of Paul to the Colossians and to Philemon.* TNTC. Leicester: Inter-Varsity, 1986.

Made in United States
Troutdale, OR
01/31/2024

17335907R00070